Patchwork Quilt Blocks in Split Ring Tatting

Karen Bovard © 2015

Published by: The ShuttleSmith Publishing Company
9102 Poppleton Avenue
Omaha, Nebraska 68124 USA

www.TheShuttleSmith.com

theshuttlesmith@gmail.com
k.bovard@yahoo.com

ISBN: 978-0-9835441-4-2

© Karen Bovard 2015 All Rights Reserved

ALL RIGHTS RESERVED. NO PART OF THIS PUBLICATION MAY BE REPRODUCED, STORED IN A RETRIEVAL SYSTEM OR TRANSMITTED IN ANY FORM BY ANY MEANS, ELECTRONIC, MECHANICAL, PHOTOCOPYING, RECORDING OR OTHERWISE WITHOUT PRIOR PERMISSION OF THE COPYRIGHT OWNERS AND PUBLISHERS.

In other words, please respect the time & talent of the author to not reproduce/share this book.

Other books by Karen Bovard / The ShuttleSmith Publishing Company

Fun with Split Ring Tatting — Karen Bovard

MORE Fun with Split Ring Tatting — Karen Bovard

Block Alphabets in Split Ring Tatting — Karen Bovard

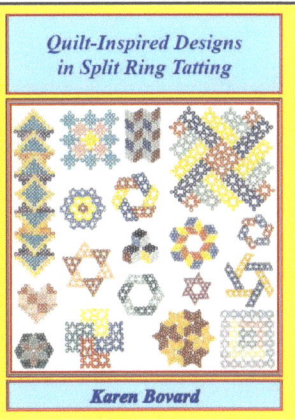
Quilt-Inspired Designs in Split Ring Tatting — Karen Bovard

INTRODUCTION

I have deliberately stayed-away from 3 artforms: bobbin lace, beading, and quilting! I will tell you that they all intrique me, I know that I would enjoy doing them. BUT I know enough about them to understand that they are all addictive, requiring much investment of time and materials to enter their world. But when I learned that the theme of the 2015 IOLI Convention was 'Lace on the Prairie', the idea of studying quilts *(a prairie woman's artform)* and converting the designs into tatting patterns was intriguing. I grew up watching my paternal grandmother quilting. It was my maternal grandmother that taught me to tat. Both these women were farm-wives on the prairie of Nebraska. I grew up on a true farm in northeast Nebraska--a true farmer's daughter. Thus, I am truly a 'lacemaker of the prairie'.

This foray into studying quilting and creating tatting designs was an enjoyable one. Quilting (like tatting) is based upon repetition and symmetry--both concepts that I find soothing in what can seem like a chaotic world. Quilting however, can allow us tatters to venture into a new world...that of COLOR. Never before have we as tatters had so many luscious colors of thread to choose from as that supplied by Handy Hands in their LizBeth thread line. At the time of this writing, there were over 160 colors in the many sizes of thread that tatters use. It seems to me that those thread colors were just waiting for a book of designs such as supplied by quilt-inspired patterns. The variegated threads even mimic printed fabric. I have been tatting for several decades and I have never really had such an opportunity to play with and put together multiple colors in one design. I am still a novice with color....some of my combinations I like, others could be better. But I am having fun with color.

All the designs in this book are based on traditional, historic quilt blocks. I did my best to get the historic name correct, but there may be other names for the same block. All designs are patchwork squares in that the finished piece is square. The color blocks are made of stacked 'square rings' (4-4-4-4) creating shapes that mimic pieces of fabric quilts: squares, triangles. However, unlike pieced fabric, more complex shapes can be tatted as one round.

A hallmark of patchwork quilts is that the block is almost always square *(as are the designs in this book)* and the use of a repeated block to produce an overall, secondary pattern. So, as space allows on the page, you will see additional illustrations comprised of 4 repeats of the basic patchwork block unit. If the original patchwork block has any degree of assymmetry, there may be more examples of a secondary design presented. Unfortunately, space does not allow me to explore all types of symmetry in this book. 'Symmetry' was an interesting side study trip for me. (For more information on the subject I would recommend the book **"Symmetry: A Design System for Quiltmakers"** by Ruth B. McDowell.)

All the designs in this book are based on traditional, historic quilt blocks. I did my best to get the historic name correct, but there may be other names for the same block. All the designs are 'Patchwork Blocks'--the finished piece is square. The color block 'pieces' are made of stacked 'square rings' (4-4-4-4) creating shapes that mimic pieces of fabric quilts: squares, triangles. However, unlike pieced fabric, more complex shapes can be tatted as one round.

Unfortunately not all the blocks have tatted-thread pieces done. I just don't have the time to tat all my designs anymore. Various talented tatters from around the country helped by tatting several designs which are located on pages 8-9. They were life-savers! Credit is given with each peice.

Many thanks to Barbara Foster at Handy Hands for donating many balls of LizBeth thread to this project. Once again another big 'Thank You' to my friend, Jennifer Bartling, for dropping everything to proof read the patterns on my 'I need it now!' schedule.

Karen Bovard/The ShuttleSmith demoing tatting at a Quilt Show

Karen Bovard is an empty-nester, newly-married tatter who lives in Omaha, Nebraska where she works full-time in a medical laboratory. When not tatting, she enjoys riding motorcycles & would love the chance to travel via motorcycle to teach at &/or attend tatting/lacemaking workshops. Note: No tattoos, piercings or leather involved.

Follow Karen Bovard on her blog & website at:
www.TheShuttleSmith.com

Karen is available to teach a variety of tatting & other lacemaking techniques.

Check out some ideas at:
http://theshuttlesmithclasses.blogspot.com/

Let Karen custom-design a class for your group that is guaranteed to challenge or just be fun.

TABLE OF CONTENTS / PATTERNS

Shoo Fly............10	**Wrench**............32
Box in a Box............11	**Broken Dishes #2**............33
Friendship Star............12-13	**Bear Paw**............34-35
Contrary Wife............14	**Sawtooth Star**............36-37
Hour Glass............15	**Hen & Chicks/Duck & Ducklings**............38-39
Bowtie............16	**Jack in the Pulpit**............40-41
Mothers Dream............17	**Whirlwind 1**............42
Pinwheel/Double Pinwheel............18-19	**Whirlwind 2**............43
Crackers............20	**Weathervane**............44-45
Churn Dash............21	**Cats Cradle**............46-47
Northstar............22-23	**Bird in the Air**............48
Broken Dishes #1............24-25	**Whirling Geese**............49
Solstice Star............26-27	**Maple Leaf**............50-51
Perpetual Motion............28	**Album**............52-53
Farmers Daughter............29	**Double Star**............54-55
Beggar Block............30	**Tulips**............56-62
Disappearing 9 Patch............31	**Walk in the Woods**............63-65

GUIDE/KEY TO *THE SHUTTLESMITH'S* VISUAL PATTERNS

The Following Standard Abbreviations are Used

R	=	Ring
SR	=	Split Ring
TOR	=	Take Off Ring/Thrown Off Ring

As in all Visual/Illustrated Patterns

- The first ring tatted that has a picot is when you will tat that picot.
- The ensuing ring tatted that is associated with that same picot will be a join.

Key Points of Illustrated/Visual Patterns

Color of Portions/Arcs
- Each color represents one of two shuttle/thread sources.

Direction of the Arcs (from Dots to Arrowhead)
- Shows which way regular rings & the portions of split rings are worked.
- Gives direction as to how the ring is to be tatted if Frontside/Backside Tatting Technique is used.
- Gives direction as to when the work is to be reversed.

Colored Letters
- Dictate which portion of a split ring is to be tatted first ('A') with regular, transferred double stitches & then the ('B') portion with untransferred, reverse-stitch double stitches.
- If a split ring does not have join or a TOR associated with it, the portions of the split ring can be tatted in any order *(colored letters will not be indicated)*.

Numbered Rings
- All the rings (regular, take off, or split ring) are numbered sequentially. The path the pattern is to be worked is to start at 'R1' & work in ascending order.

Regular Rings in Visual Patterns--Including Take Off Rings

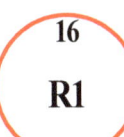

-- The <u>dot</u> designates the starting point of the ring ●
-- The <u>arrowhead</u> designates the ending point of the ring. ◄ *(A regular ring starts & ends at the same point.)*
-- '**R**' is used to designate a (regular) ring.
-- The larger '#'/number (after the 'R') designates the order in which the rings are tatted & thus how the pattern is worked.
-- The smaller '#'/number on the inside of the arc is the number of double stitches in the ring or in that particular portion of the ring between picots and joins.

A regular-tatted ring in Visual Pattern style is distinguished by the fact that:
- There is only 1 arc.
- There is only 1 color used for the arc, starting dot, & ending arrowhead.
- The starting point & the ending point are at the same place on the ring.

Split Rings in Visual Patterns

-- 2 <u>dots</u> of different colors designate the starting points of the 2 different thread sources of the split ring.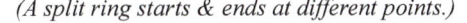
-- 2 <u>arrowheads</u> of different colors designate the ending points of the 2 thread sources of the split ring.
(A split ring starts & ends at different points.)
-- The <u>arcs</u> represent the two thread sources that create split rings.
(When you see a ring diagram with 2 colors used, you know that it is a split ring.)
-- The abbreviations '**SR**' are used: the '**S**' meaning 'Split' & the '**R**' meaning 'Ring'.
-- The larger '#'/number (after the 'R') designates the order in which the rings are tatted and thus how the pattern is worked.
-- The '#'/number on the inside of the arcs is the number of double stitches in the ring or in that particular portion of the ring between picots & joins.

Numbered Rings--Path of the Pattern

-- How the pattern is worked (or the 'path') is designated in Visual Patterns by the number inside the rings next to either **R**, **SR**, or **TOR**.
-- Start at R1 and then progress numerically (1 then 2, then 3, then 4.....) through the pattern.
-- There may be different ways or paths to take to tat the pattern other than the one illustrated. However, the patterns have been carefully designed & charted to lessen the complexity of the pattern & to allow for the following conditions:
  - The pattern can be worked continuously, from start to end, in one round or as few rounds as possible.
  - Regular joins *(not Split Ring Joining Technique)* can be used.
    -- Regular joins can only be made on the ***first*** portion of a split ring *(the regular, transferred double stitches)*.
  - Take off rings (TOR's) can be created without the need for an additional thread source.
    -- TOR's are created on the ***second*** portion of the split ring *(the untransferred, reverse-stitch double stitches)*.
    -- TOR's *(which are regular rings)* allow regular joins to be used.
  - Regular rings are used as often as possible.

COLORED LETTERS IN VISUAL PATTERNS

-- Some of the split rings in the visual patterns will have colored letter designations (*inside the ring, and next to the stitch count*) and some will not.
-- If a split ring does not have a join or take off ring associated with it, the portions of the split ring can be tatted in any order.

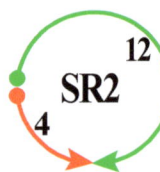

This split ring pattern can be tatted in one of two ways--either choice appropriate:
1. The 12-stitch (green) portion can be tatted first with regular, transferred stitches and then the 4-stitch (red) portion is tatted with reverse, untransferred double stitches.   **OR**
2. Tat the 4-stitch (red) portion first with regular, transferred stitches and then the 12-stitch (green) portion is tatted with reverse, untransferred stitches.

However, the order in which the split ring portions are tatted in some split rings is important for two reasons:
1. To create joins utilizing traditonal tatting joining technique--NOT Split Ring Joining Technique (*which is more cumbersome to master and does not create as 'neat' a join*).
    -- Done from the **first portion** (the regular, transferred double stitches)
2. To be able to create Take-Off Rings (TOR's) without the need to use a third thread source.
    -- Done from the **second portion** (the reverse, untransferred double stitches)

This split ring pattern dictates that the 12-stitch (green) be tatted first with regular, transferred stitches and then the 4-stitch (red) portion is tatted with reverse, untransferred double stitches.

Just like in the alphabet, 'A' comes before 'B' and thus the 'A' portion is done first.

DIRECTION OF THE LINE ARCS (FROM DOT TO ARROWHEADS)

-- Shows the direction that the ring is worked.
-- Shows which way regular rings and the portions of split rings are worked.
-- Gives clues/direction to how the ring is to be tatted if Frontside/Backside Tatting technique is used.
    -- If the arc of a regular ring is '*clockwise*' then the ring is tatted as a '*frontside*' ring.
    -- If the arc of a regular ring is '*counter-clockwise*' then the ring is tatted as a '*backside*' ring.

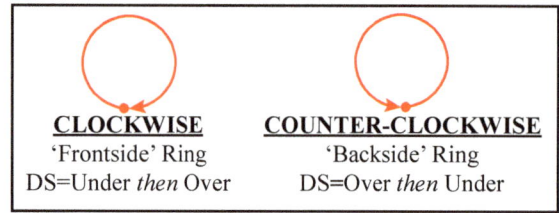

In split rings, both clockwise and counter-clockwise arcs/portions are part of each split ring.

The direction of the first portion of the split ring made dictates whether the split ring is tatted as either a 'frontside' or a 'backside' ring.
-If Portion A is '*clockwise*' then the split ring is tatted as a '*frontside*' ring
-If Portion A is '*counter-clockwise*' then the the split ring is tatted as a '*backside*' ring

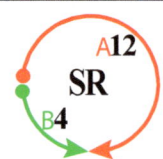

CLOCKWISE First
'Frontside' Ring
With the 'Red' shuttle make 12 regular, transferred double stitches: ***Under-Stitch-first; followed by Over Stitch***

With the 'Green' shuttle make 4 reverse, untransferred double stitches: ***Over Stitch-first; followed by Under Stitch***

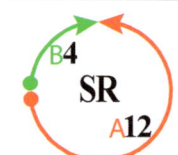

COUNTER-CLOCKWISE First
'Backside' Ring
With the 'Red' shuttle make 12 regular, transferred double stitches: ***Over-Stitch-first; followed by Under Stitch***

With the 'Green' shuttle make 4 reverse, untransferred double stitches: ***Under Stitch-first; followed by Over Stitch***

-- Gives visual clues/direction as to when the work is to be reversed. (*Illustrated patterns do NOT give written directions as to when to Reverse Work.*)

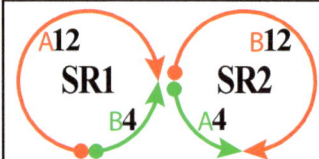

If you tat one ring as a 'frontside' element (*the first portion of the split ring &/or the regular ring is a clockwise arc--***SR1**) and then the second ring is a 'backside' element (*the first portion of the split ring &/or the regular ring is a counter-clockwise arc--***SR2**) you will need to Reverse Work between these two rings.

Take Off/Thrown Off Rings (TOR)

--A Take Off/Thrown Off Ring is a 'regular' ring that is created/tatted in the middle of another element. In traditional tatting (rings/chains/no split rings) a Take Off Ring would have been referred to as a 'second-shuttle element' because is was tatted in the middle of a chain element & necessitated the use of a second shuttle. In the case of the patterns in this book, it is made in steps while tatting a Split Ring.

--Take Off Rings allow rings to be tatted that otherwise would have been unable to be tatted/'orphaned'.

--Take Off Rings can be done from either portion of the split ring. If they arise from the first/transferred double stitch portion of the split ring, the thread source to tat the Take Off Ring must come from a third shuttle/thread source & be carried along the ring thread inside the double stitches *(known as Padded Tatting Technique)*. Take Off Rings can be made, without the need for a third thread source, if they are made from the second, untransferred stitch portion of the split ring.

--The patterns in this book were carefully charted so that if you follow the path/plan of the pattern, tatting the split ring portions in the order they are illustrated--*colored A's & B's*, you can tat Take Off Rings using only two thread sources.

--Take Off Rings are tatted as a 'unit', in steps with the split ring it is associated with.

A TOR is tatted as a 'unit', in steps, with the SR it is associated with:

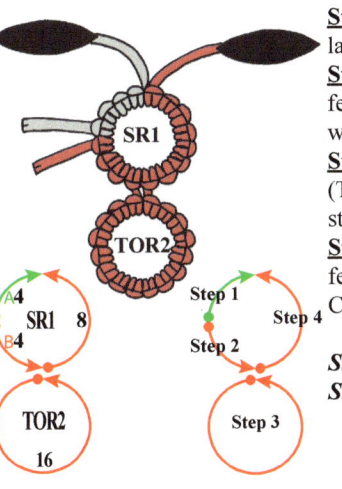

Step 1 With Shuttle A form a ring & make 4 regular, transferred double stitches.
Step 2 With Shuttle B make 4 reverse, untransferred double stitches on the ring thread. Reverse work.
Step 3 With Shuttle B--tat Take Off Ring 2 (TOR2): make 16 regular, transferred double stitches. Close TOR2. Reverse work.
Step 4 With Shuttle B make 8 reverse, untransferred double stitches on the ring thread. Close Split Ring 1 by pulling Shuttle A thread.

Steps 1, 2, & 4 create the split ring.
Step 3 creates the take off ring.

More than one Take Off Ring can be make from a single split ring.

This illustration shows a split ring (#2) with 3 Take Off Rings (#3, 4, 5). Rings #1 & 6 are tatted as regular rings.

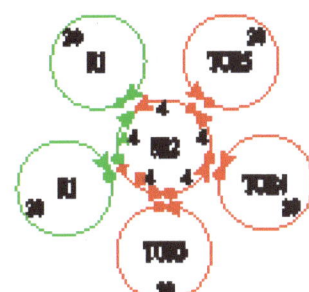

All the Rings in this Book are Designed to be Round-Shaped

-Close the ring by pulling the working shuttle/thread downward, away from the base of the ring.
-Use your fingers to push the ring into a round-shape.

All Rings are Tatted with No-Space of Thread Between Rings

-The visual effect of the pieces in this book is that each ring is closely adjacent to its neighboring ring(s).
-All rings are started as close to one another as possible. NO 'gaposis'!!!

Picot Size--Use of Joining Picots

-The pieces were designed with the idea that all the rings lie in close relationship with one another.
-The picots used in this book/style of tatting are all examples of Joining Picots.
-Joining picots are minute picots that barely allow for insertion of a tiny crochet hook. They are used only for joining, not as ornamental picots. A Joining Picot is barely recognizable as a picot loop.
-A space of thread between the two double stitches that is creating the properly-sized Joining Picot is equal to one double stitch width.
-In the process of facilitating very tight joins between rings, very small joining picots are created. A small-gauge crochet hook is necessary to facilitate these joins.
-Proper Joining Picot size is actually so small that at times it maybe difficult to get even a tiny crochet hook into the picot loop to use it. At these times, a dental-pick tool or a blunt-tipped sewing needle *(such as a Tapestry needle--ca. Size 20, 22, or 24)* is useful to pull the picots out to a sufficient size to be able to insert a joining hook to facilitate the join.
-If you forgot to create a picot, all hope is not lost! Just insert your crochet hook or pick/needle between the stitches where the picot 'should be'. Pull out this horizontal space of thread and use it as a picot. Picots formed this way will be an appropriate size for joining the patterns tatted in this book.

Frontside/Backside Joining Technique

Because these Quilt-Inspired Designs in Split Ring Tatting utilize tatted blocks in different colors, use of Frontside/Backside (FS/BS) Joining Technique is encouraged even if you choose not to use FS/BS Tatting Technique.

The act of making a regular *(sliding, not locking)* join adds an extra horizontal thread to the stitches being tatted. This horizontal thread is the picot you are joining to. If the joining picot is a different color than the ring element you are joining to, then this horizontal thread will show as a 'bleb' of color. It must be managed with Joining Technique/Strategy to not be visually distracting.

Even if you choose not to practice/use Frontside/Backside Tatting Technique, you will need to choose one side of your work to be the backside. By choosing which Joining Technique to use (**Up Join** or **Down Join**) you can manipulate all the horizontal thread spaces of a join to show on one side *(the 'backside')* of the work. This is mainly only important when joining different colored rings together *(such as between the different blocks that make up a quilt block or when utilizing variegated thread within a single block.)*

There are two joining techniques. Both techniques join two elements together. How and when they are used can produce different visual effects due to where the extra horizontal thread (from the picot) ends up--either on the front or backside of the elements.

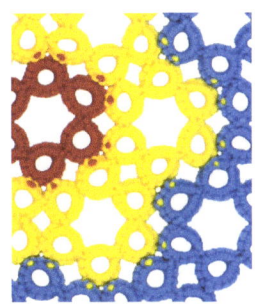

'Backside' view: You can see the red joining picots in the yellow round & the yellow joining picots in the blue round.

Up Join

This is what is regarded as the Traditional Join.

How to work: --Lay the picot **on top** of the working thread of the ring you are joining together.
--The working thread is brought **UP** and through the picot, the shuttle passed through the loop of thread formed, and the join nestled/tensioned down into position.

The result: The horizontal thread (supplied by the picot) is on the **backside** of the work.

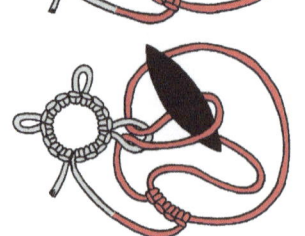

This join is sometimes called a 'Frontside Join' because the horizontal space of thread is toward the 'backside' of the piece/element and does not distract from the 'frontside' of the work. In other words, the 'frontside' is visually preserved.

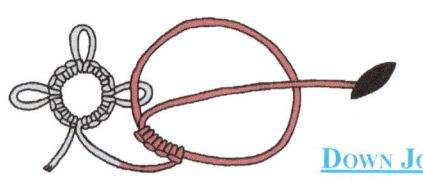

Down Join

This is a relatively new joining technique.

How to work: --Lay the picot **below** the working thread of the ring you are joining together.
--The working thread is brought **DOWN** and through the picot, the shuttle passed through the loop of thread formed, and the join nestled/tensioned down into position.

The result: The horizontal thread (supplied by the picot) is on the **frontside** of the work.

Simplification of WHICH Join to Use

Remembering which join (Up vs Down) to use can be daunting. So I have come up with this mental/physical approach to Frontside/Backside Joining Technique.

First: You must decide which side will be your frontside vs. backside....then stick to this plan.

-Lay the working thread on the 'backside' of the joining picot.
-Insert the crochet hook/joining device in the 'frontside' of the picot
-Bring the loop of working thread to the 'frontside' of the piece and insert shuttle through this loop to capture the join, tensioning the join as ususal.

The key point to remember is: Always insert the crochet hook/joining device into the 'frontside' of the picot then bring the loop of thread toward the 'frontside' of the work = you will position the horizontal space of thread to the 'backside' of the piece.

Step by Step Instructions as to How to Read *The ShuttleSmith's* Visual Patterns

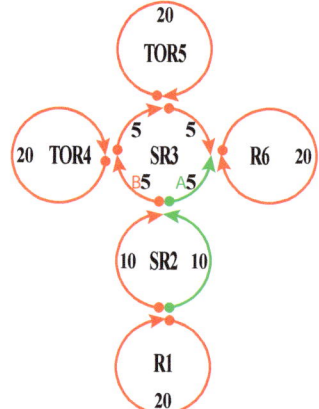

Ring 1 is a regularly-tatted ring. Only one shuttle/thread source is needed. Tat 20 regular, transferred double stitches and then close the ring.

The next ring in Split Ring 2 (SR2). It is an example of an 'even' split ring. To tat this ring, you will need a second shuttle/thread source. Since no colored letters are used in this illustration, either portion (the green or the red shuttle/thread source) can be tatted first/second. One way to create this split ring is to use the red shuttle/thread source to tat 10 regular, transferred double stitches. Then use the green shuttle/thread source to tat 10 reverse, untransferred double stitches. Close the ring by pulling the red shuttle/thread source.

Ring #3 is an uneven split ring (SR3) with two take-off rings associated with it (TOR4 & TOR5). These 3 rings (SR3, TOR4, & TOR5) are tatted as a unit in 6 steps:

Step 1: With the green shuttle/thread source tat 5 regular, transferred double stitches. You know to use this shuttle/thread source because of the colored letter 'A' associated with this portion of the split ring.
Step 2: With the red shuttle/thread source tat 5 reverse, untransferred double stitches.
Step 3: Take Split Ring 3 off your hand. Reverse work. With the red shuttle/thread tat Take Off Ring 4 as a regular ring of 20 transferrred double stitches. Close Take Off Ring 4. Reverse work.
Step 4: Put Split Ring 3 back onto your hand. With the red shuttle thread source tat 5 more reverse, untransferred double stitches.
Step 5: Take Split Ring 3 off your hand. Reverse work. With the red shuttle/thread tat Take Off Ring 5 as a regular ring of 20 transferrred double stitches. Close Take Off Ring 5. Reverse work.
Step 6: Put Split Ring 3 back onto your hand. With the red shuttle thread source tat 5 more reverse, unstransferred double stitches. Close Split Ring 3 by pulling the green shuttle/thread source.

Ring #6 is a regular tatted ring. Only one shuttle/thread source is needed. Either thread source can be used. To follow the illustration, use the red shuttle/thread source to tat 20 regular, transferred double stitches, then close the ring.

Notes on direction of the arcs of the rings & their various portions and relationship to Frontside/Back Tatting Technique & Reverse Work:
- R1: the red arc is clockwise--this is a 'frontside' ring.
- SR2: depend upon which shuttle/thread source is used first. If the red shuttle/thread source is used for the first step/portion of the split ring then the arc is clockwise, thus it is a 'frontside' ring. Both portions are tatted the same way--as 'frontside' stitches. However, if the green shuttle/thread source is used first, the arc of this portion is counter-clockwise, thus the entire split ring would be tatted as a 'backside' ring.
- SR3 directs you to tat the green shuttle/thread source first. Since this arc is counter-clockwise the entire split ring would be tatted as a 'backside' ring.
- TOR4, TOR5, & R6 are all clockwise & thus are 'frontside' rings using the red shuttle/thread source.
- Because SR3 is a 'backside' ring and then TOR 4/5 are 'frontside' rings, you will need to Reverse Work when going from SR3 to TOR4 (Same for SR3 to TOR5). Another Reverse Work is needed when going from SR3 (a 'backside' ring) to R6 (a 'frontside' ring).

APPROACH TO WORKING PATCHWORK QUILT BLOCK PATTERNS

Quilt-Inspired Split Ring Tatting patterns like historic, fabric quilts have symmetry. Instead of every patchwork block being a separate pattern, the following patterns are constructed usually from the center outward. The patchwork block design is tatted in 'rounds' as directed by the numbers. Each separate block/round has a number. Start tatting block #1, then block #2, & so on. Blocks of the same size/shape/attachment will have the same pattern. These patterns are designated by the capital letters. This approach is taken to simplify the pattern process as well as minimize the number of patterns needed. If each block had its own pattern this book would be much larger or feature fewer patterns.

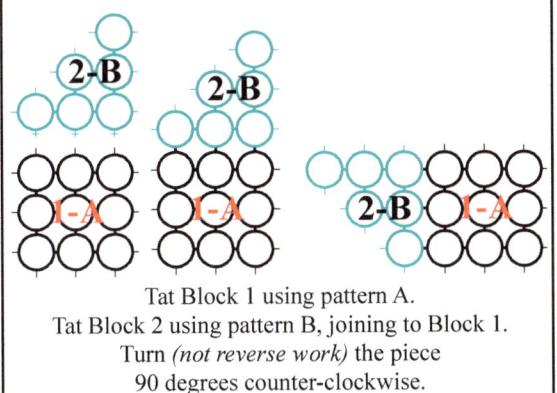

Tat Block 1 using pattern A.
Tat Block 2 using pattern B, joining to Block 1.
Turn *(not reverse work)* the piece
90 degrees counter-clockwise.

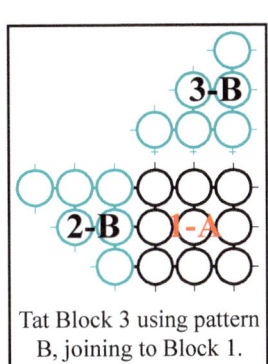

Tat Block 3 using pattern B, joining to Block 1.

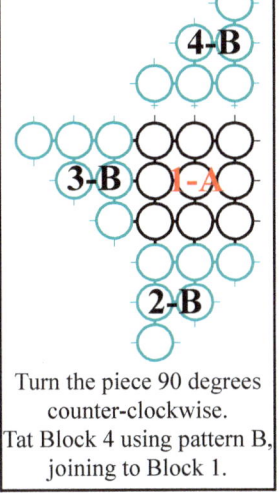

Turn the piece 90 degrees counter-clockwise.
Tat Block 4 using pattern B, joining to Block 1.

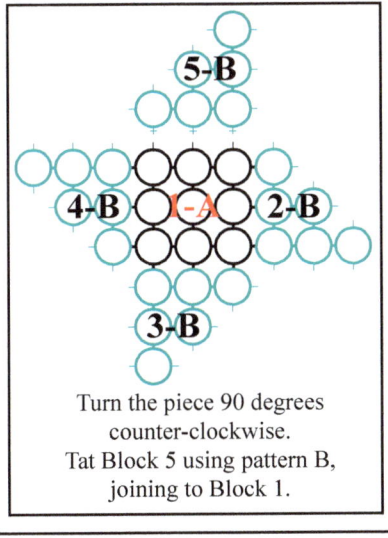

Turn the piece 90 degrees counter-clockwise.
Tat Block 5 using pattern B, joining to Block 1.

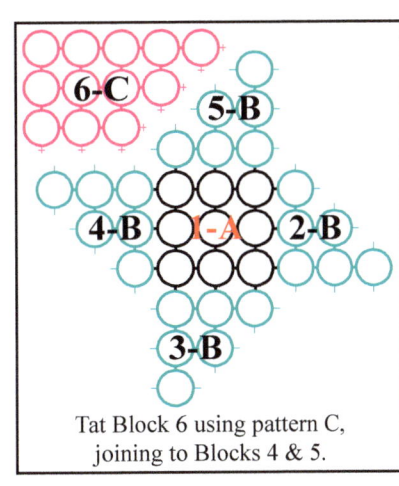

Tat Block 6 using pattern C, joining to Blocks 4 & 5.

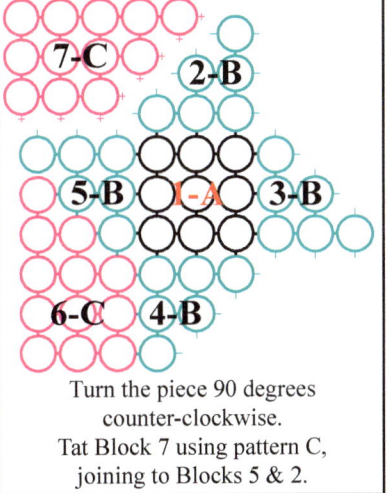

Turn the piece 90 degrees counter-clockwise.
Tat Block 7 using pattern C, joining to Blocks 5 & 2.

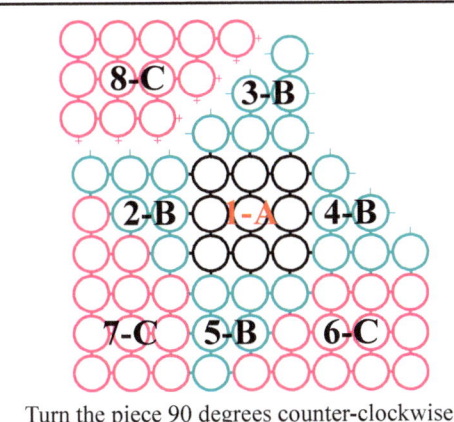

Turn the piece 90 degrees counter-clockwise.
Tat Block 8 using pattern C, joining to Blocks 2 & 3.

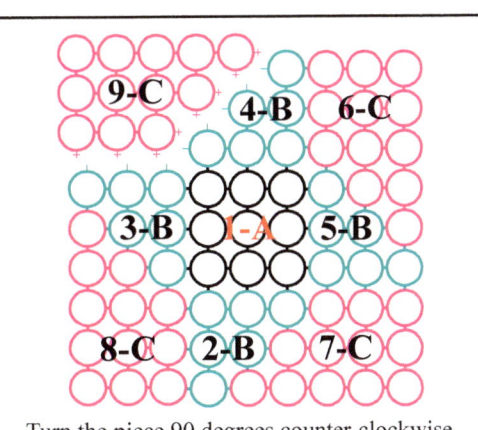

Turn the piece 90 degrees counter-clockwise.
Tat Block 9 using pattern C, joining to Blocks 3 & 4.

Disappearing 9 Patch
Kim Wallace

Perpetual Motion
Karen Bovard

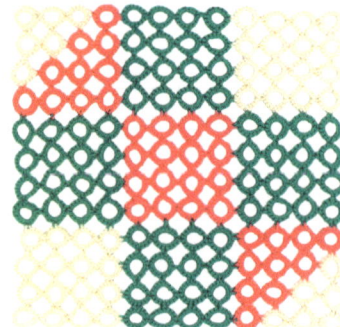
Hour Glass
Sunela Thomas

Bird in the Air
Shannon Campos-Hatfield

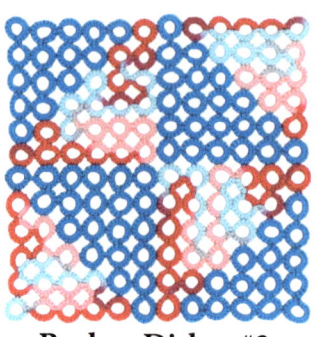
Broken Dishes #2
Phyllis Schmidt

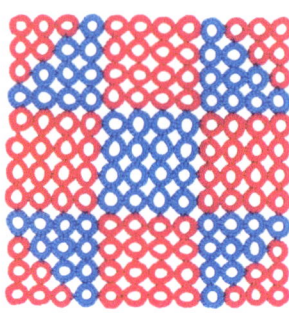
Shoo Fly
Shannon Campos-Hatfield

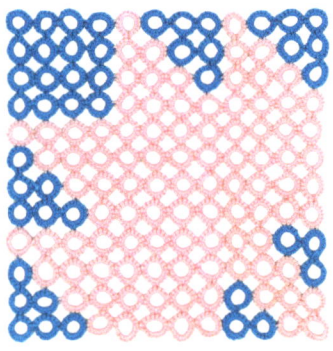
Maple Leaf
Phyllis Schmidt

Crackers
Shannon Campos-Hatfield

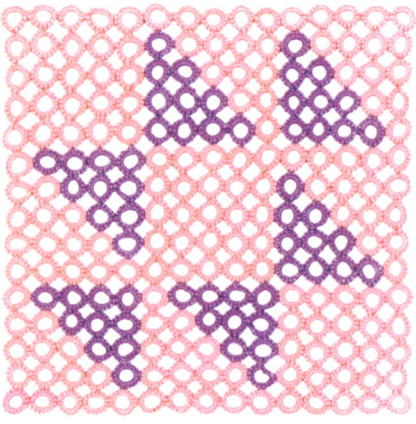
Cats Cradle
Phyllis Schmidt

Beggar Block
Sunela Thomas

Walk in the Woods
Kristen Fink

Bowtie
Phyllis Schmidt

Double Pinwheel
Karen Bovard

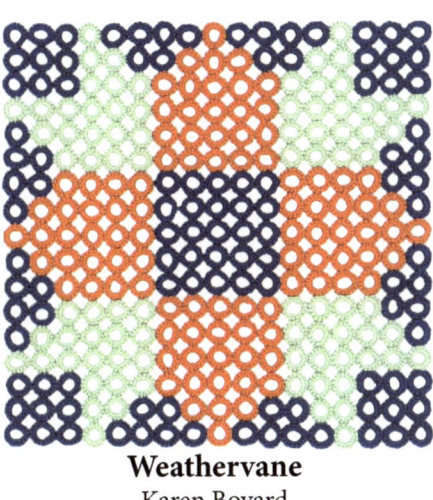
Whirlwind 2
Kim Wallace

Weathervane
Karen Bovard

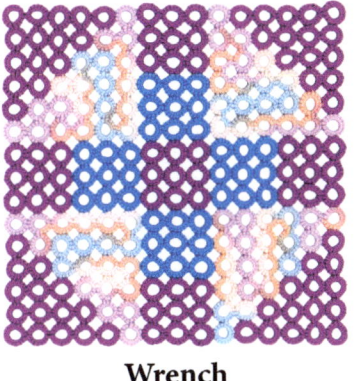
Wrench
Karen Bovard

Beggar Block
Shannon Campos-Hatfield

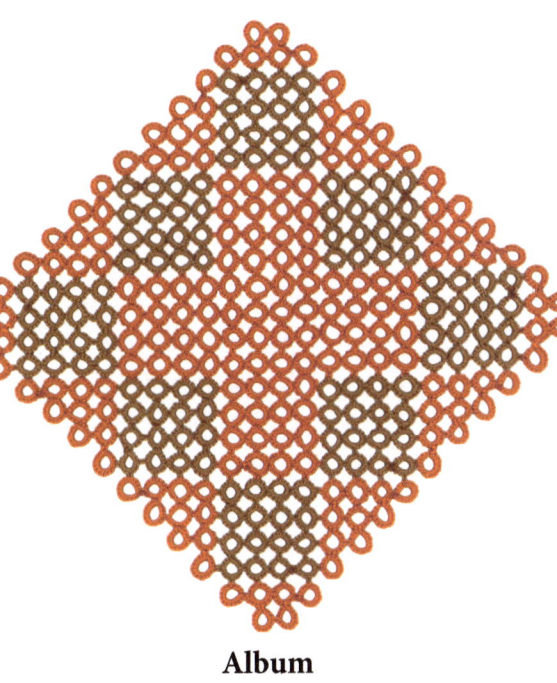
Album
Patricia Greninger

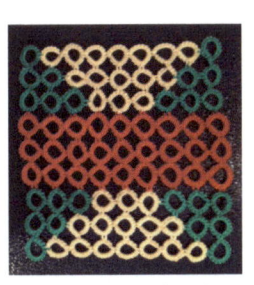
Beggar Block
Sunela Thomas

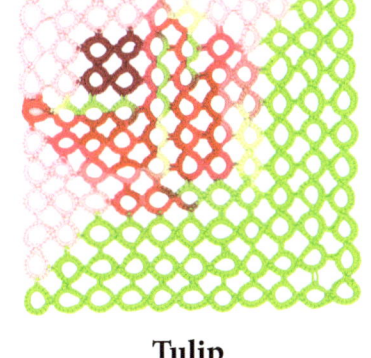
Tulip
Tara Johnson

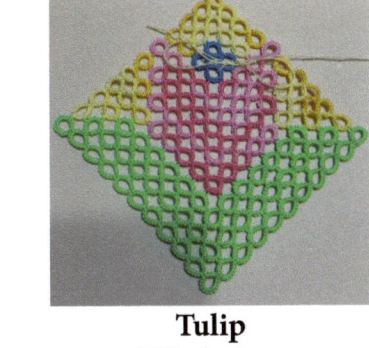
Box in a Box
Anitra Stone

Tulip
Waleska Sosa

Tulip
Waleska Sosa

Shoo Fly

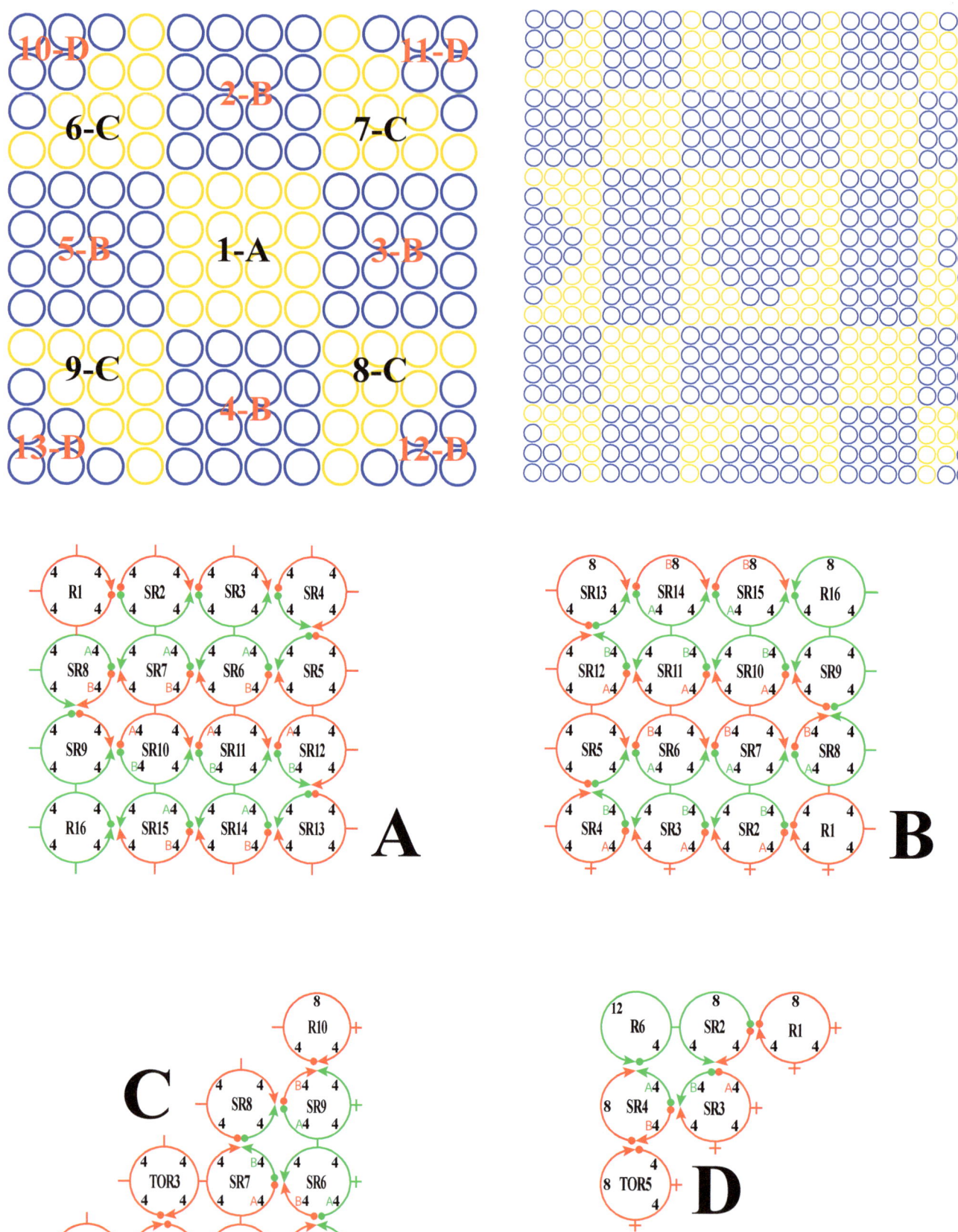

Box in a Box

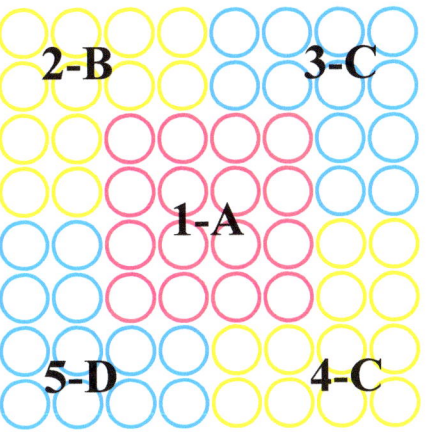
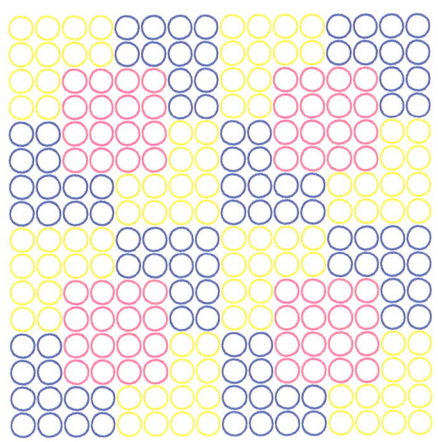

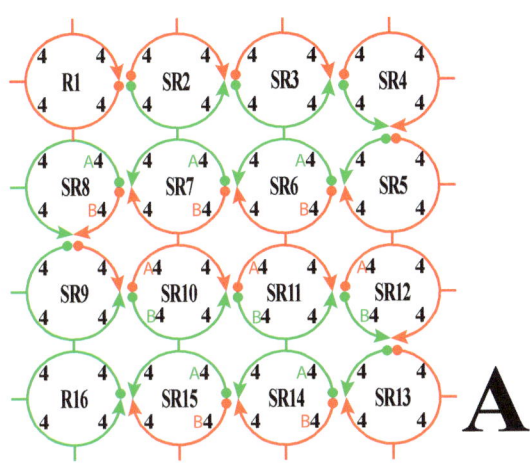

A

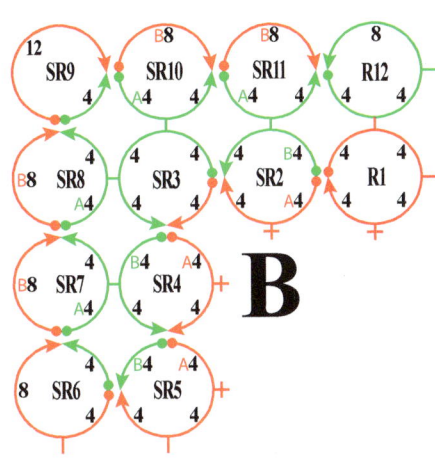

B

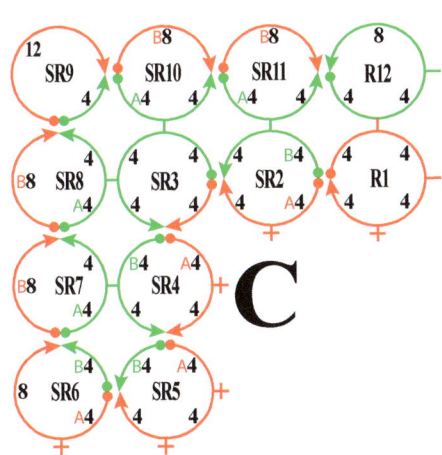

C

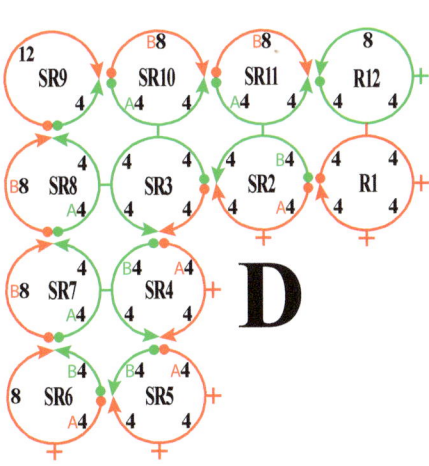

D

11

Friendship Star

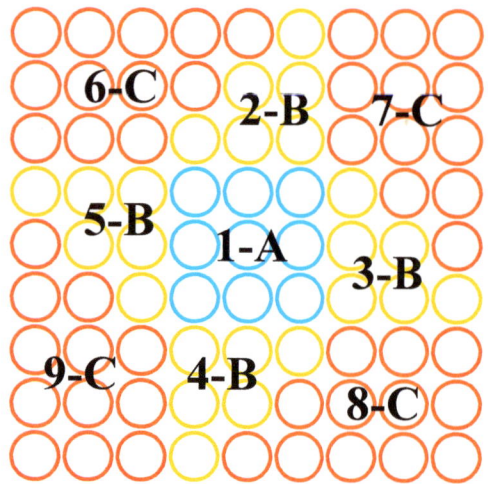

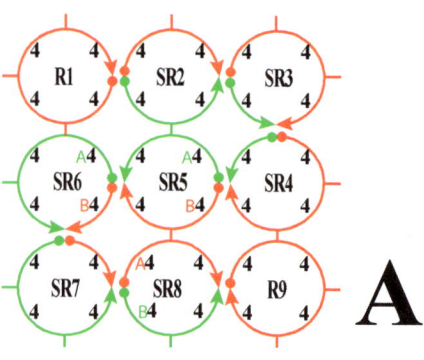
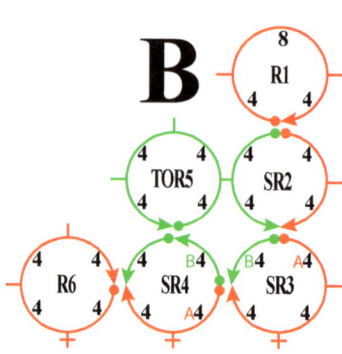
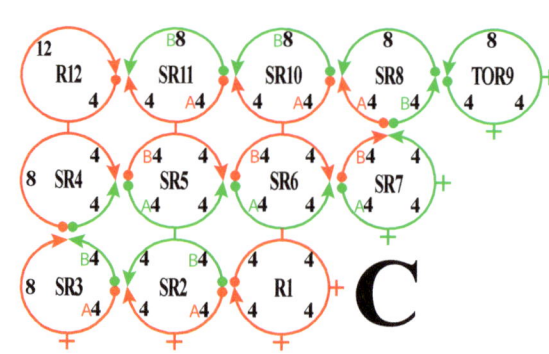

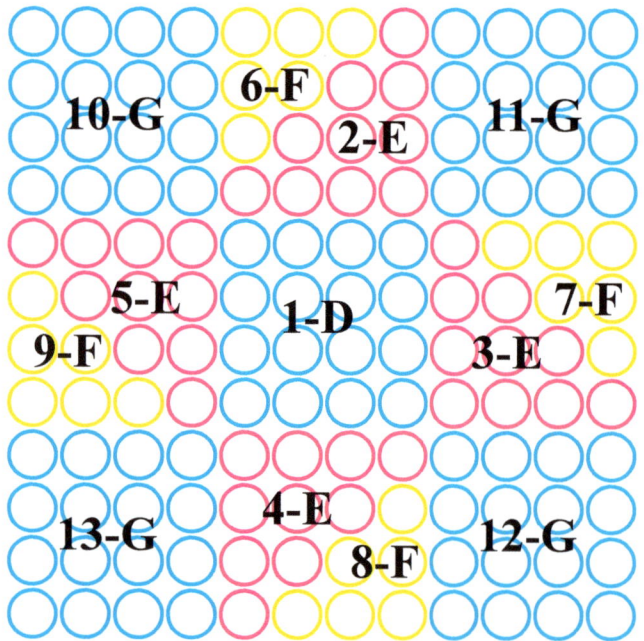
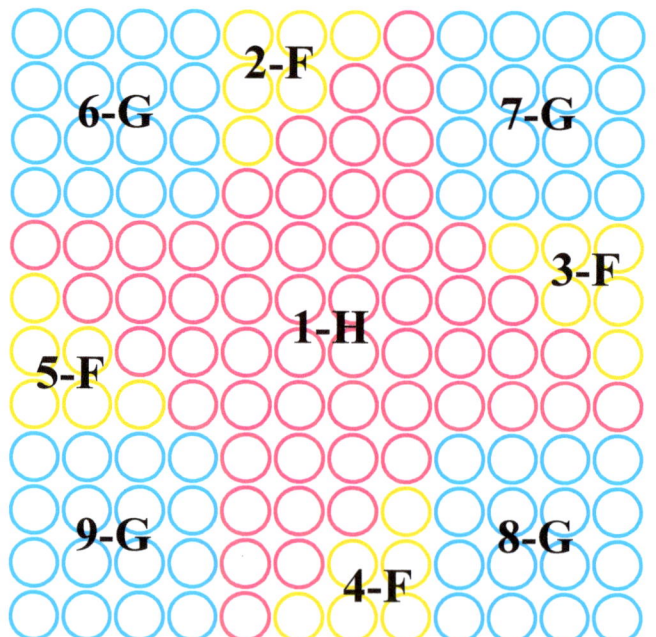

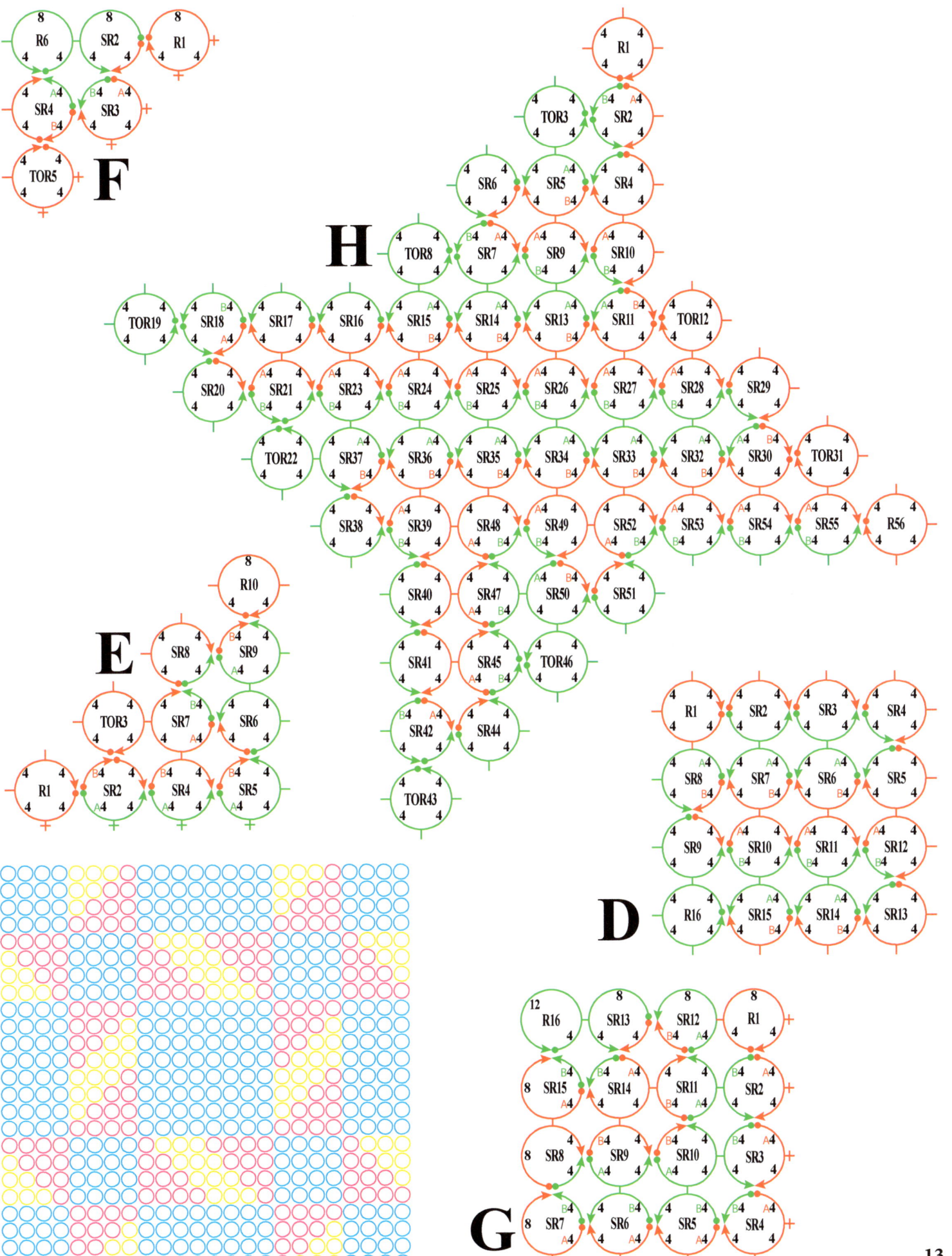

Contrary Wife

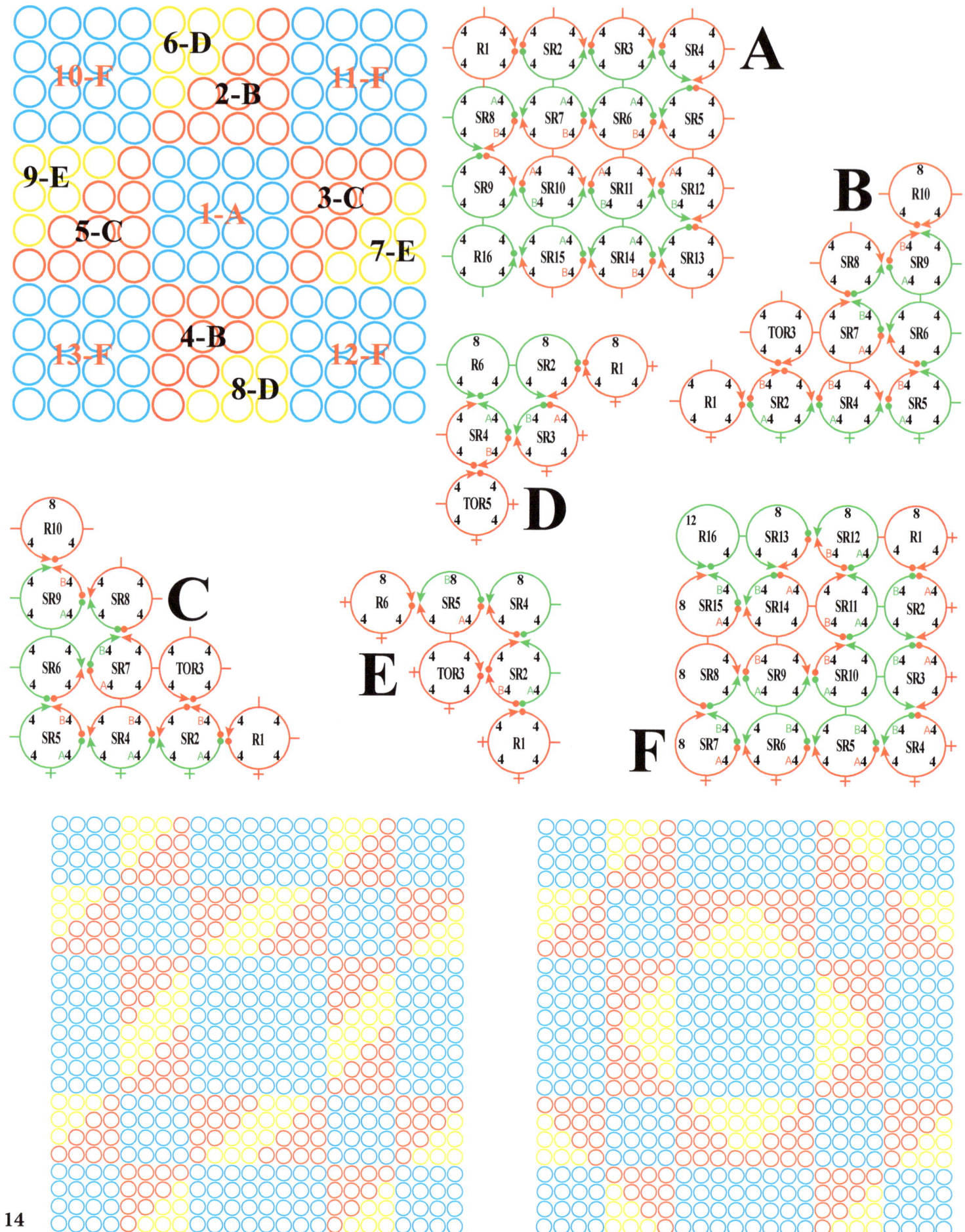

Hour Glass

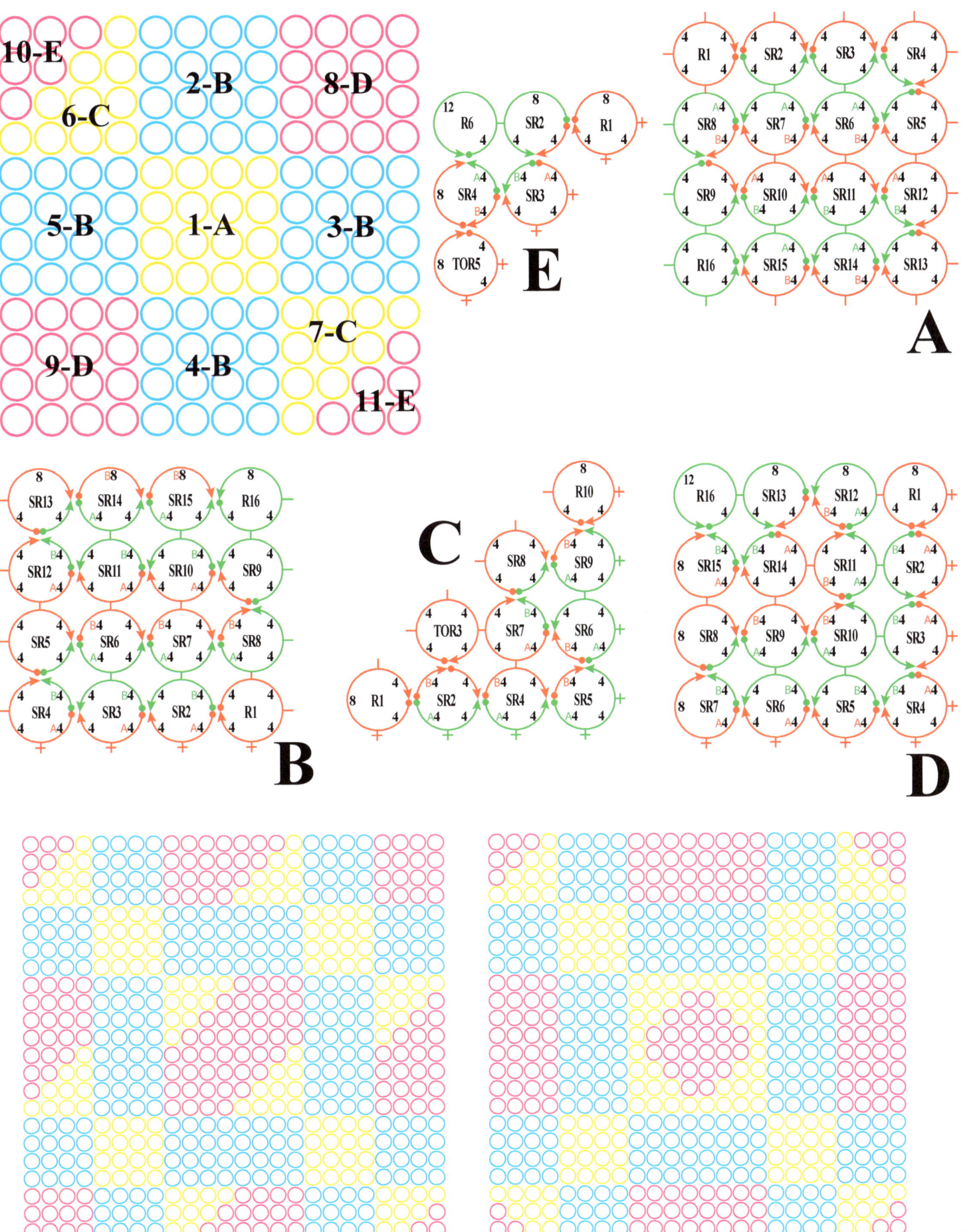

Bowtie

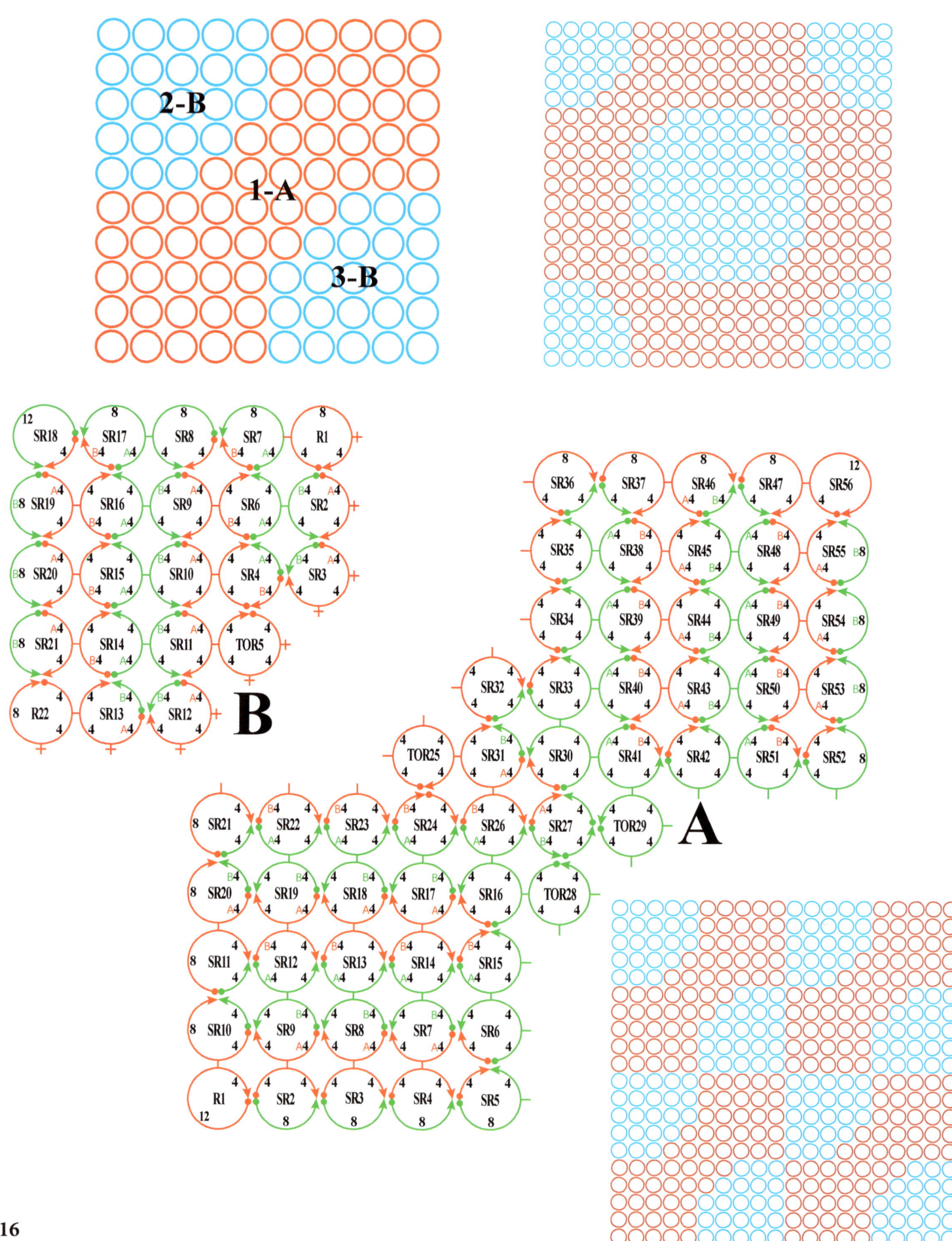

Mothers Dream

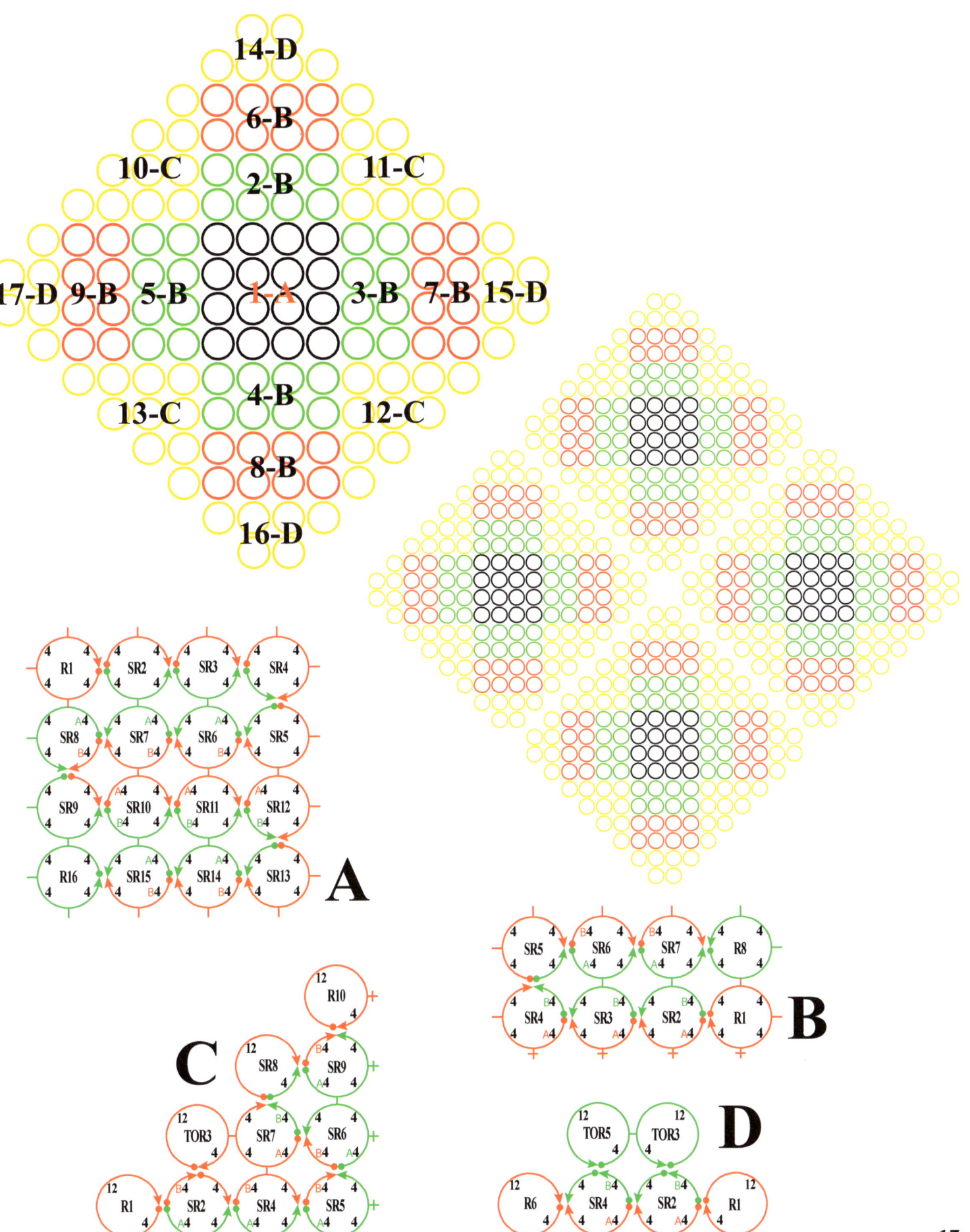

Pinwheel

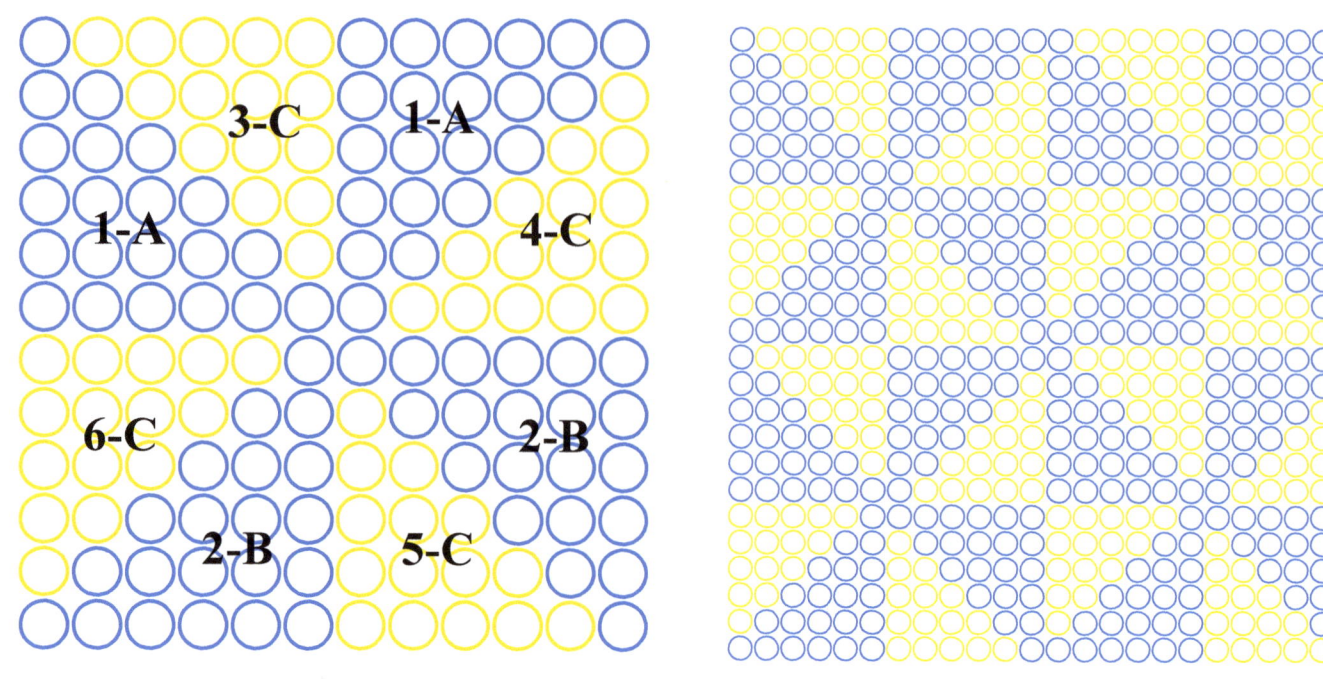

Double Pinwheel

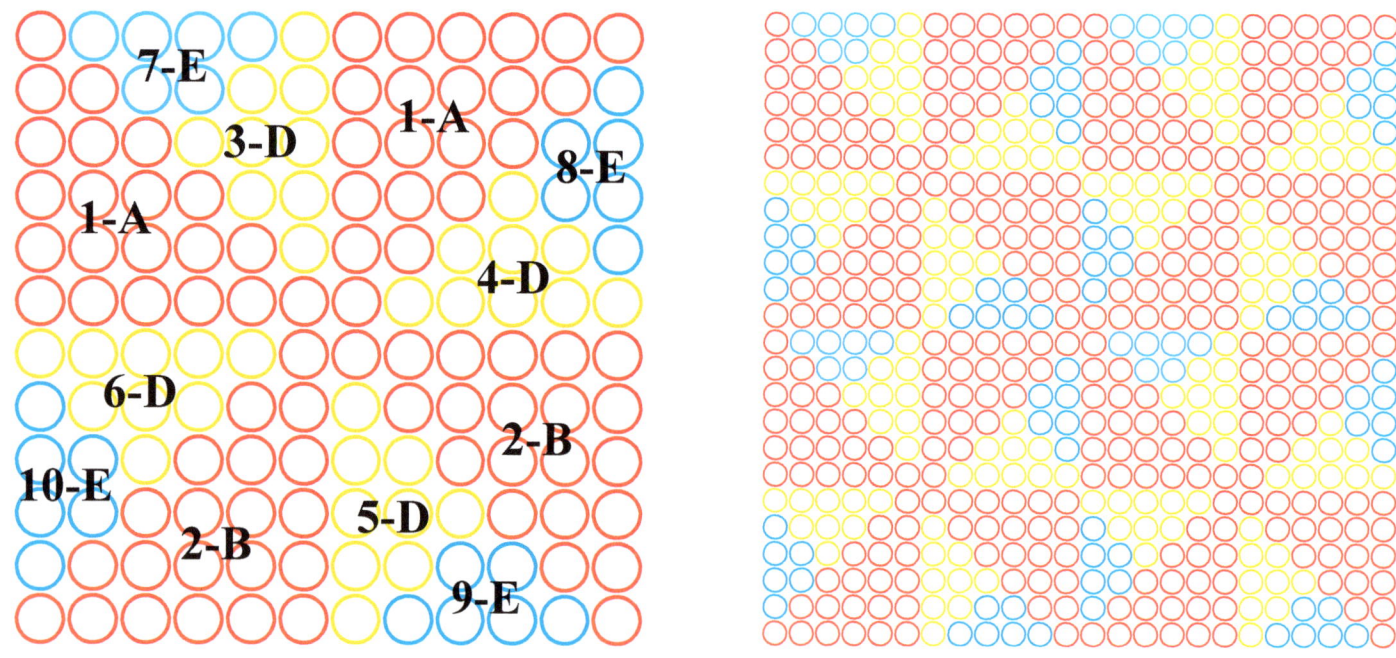

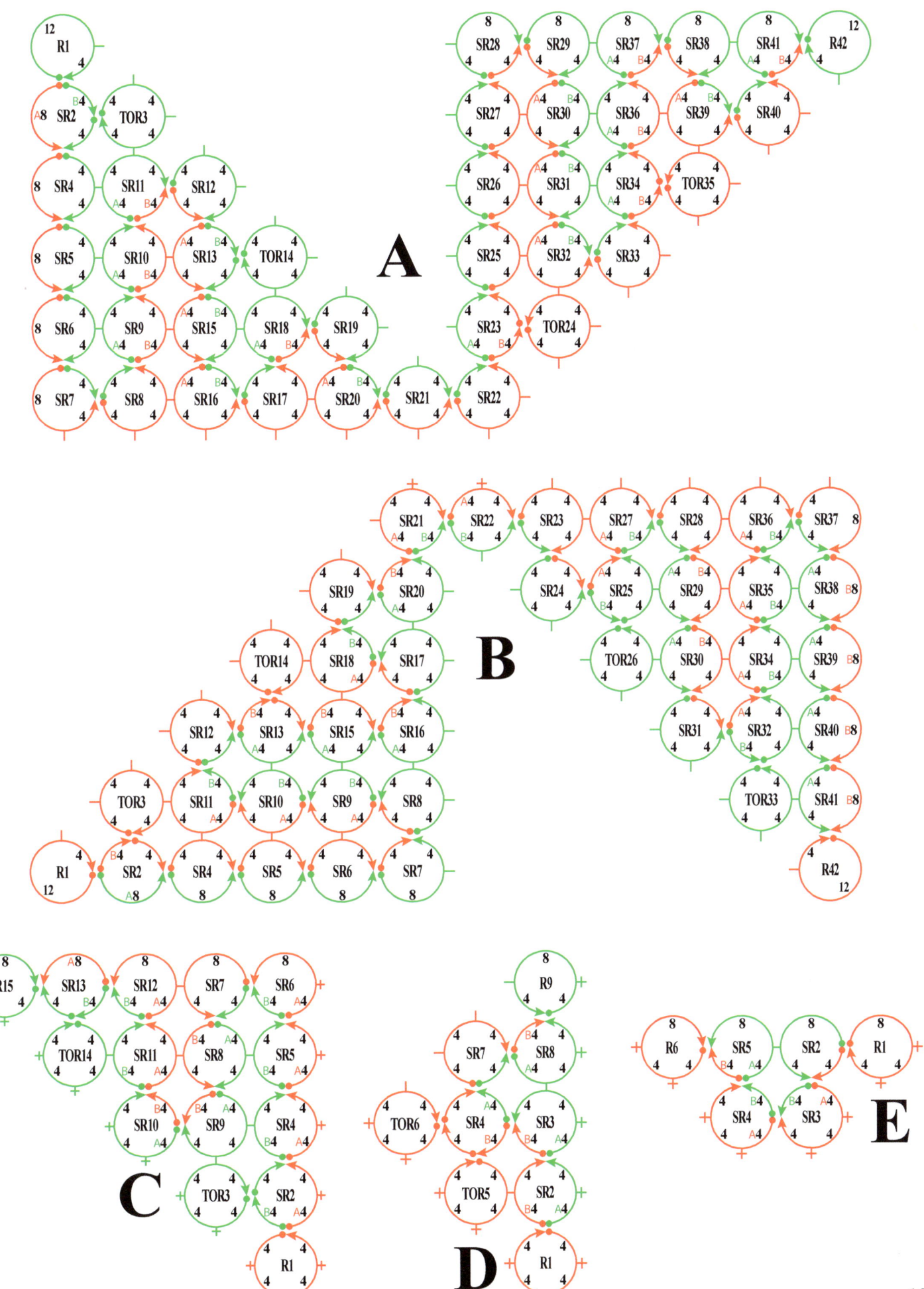

Crackers

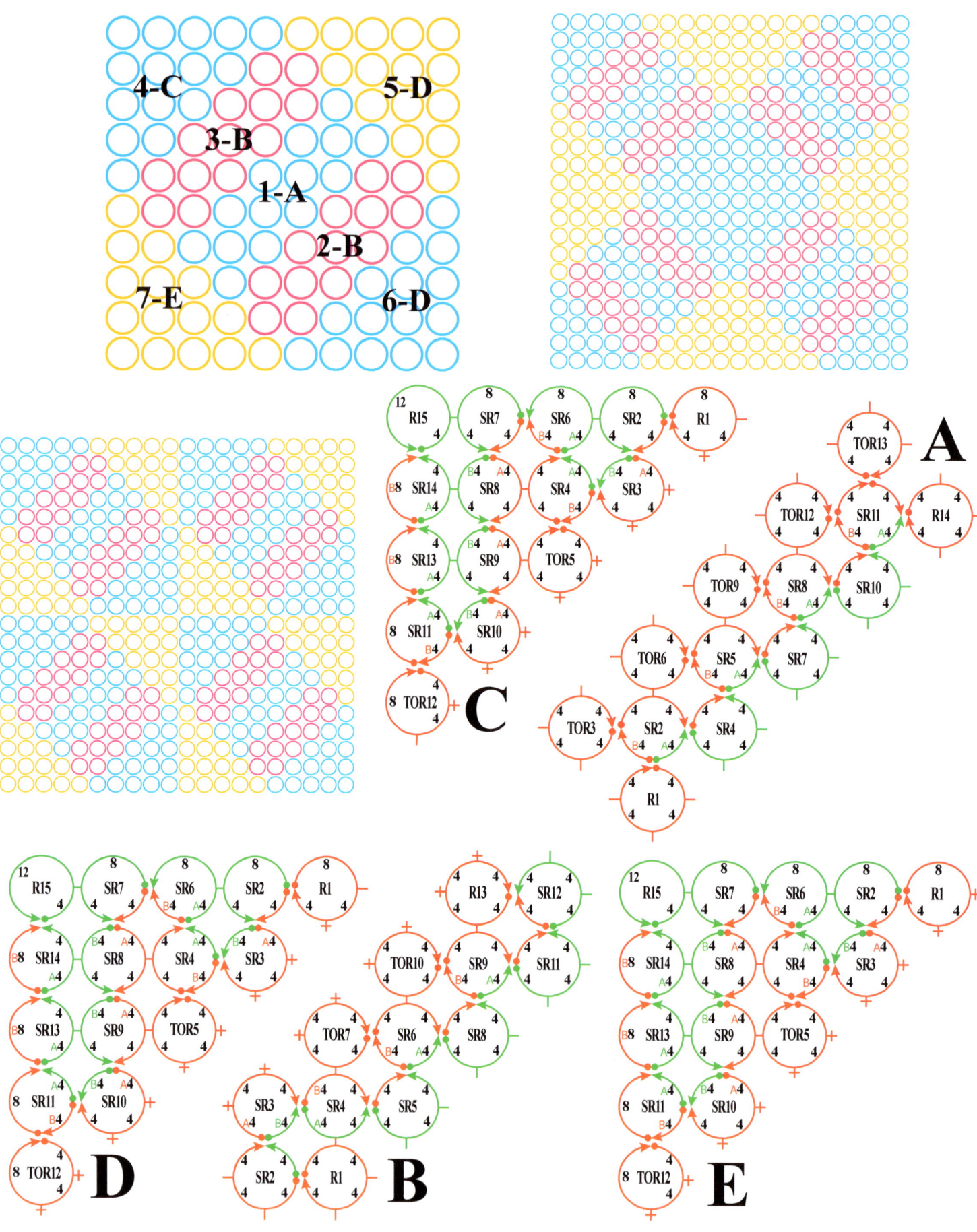

Churn Dash

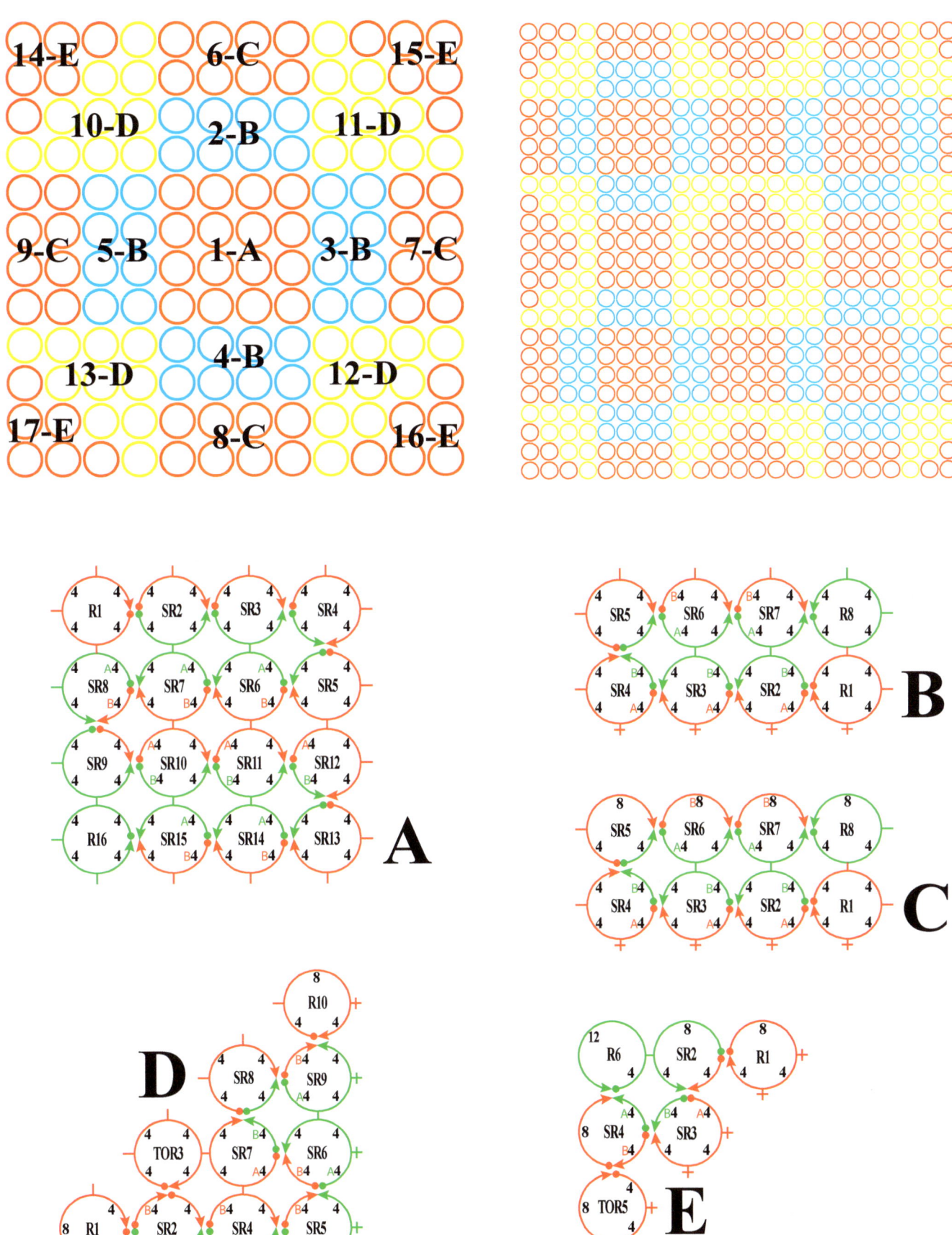

North Star

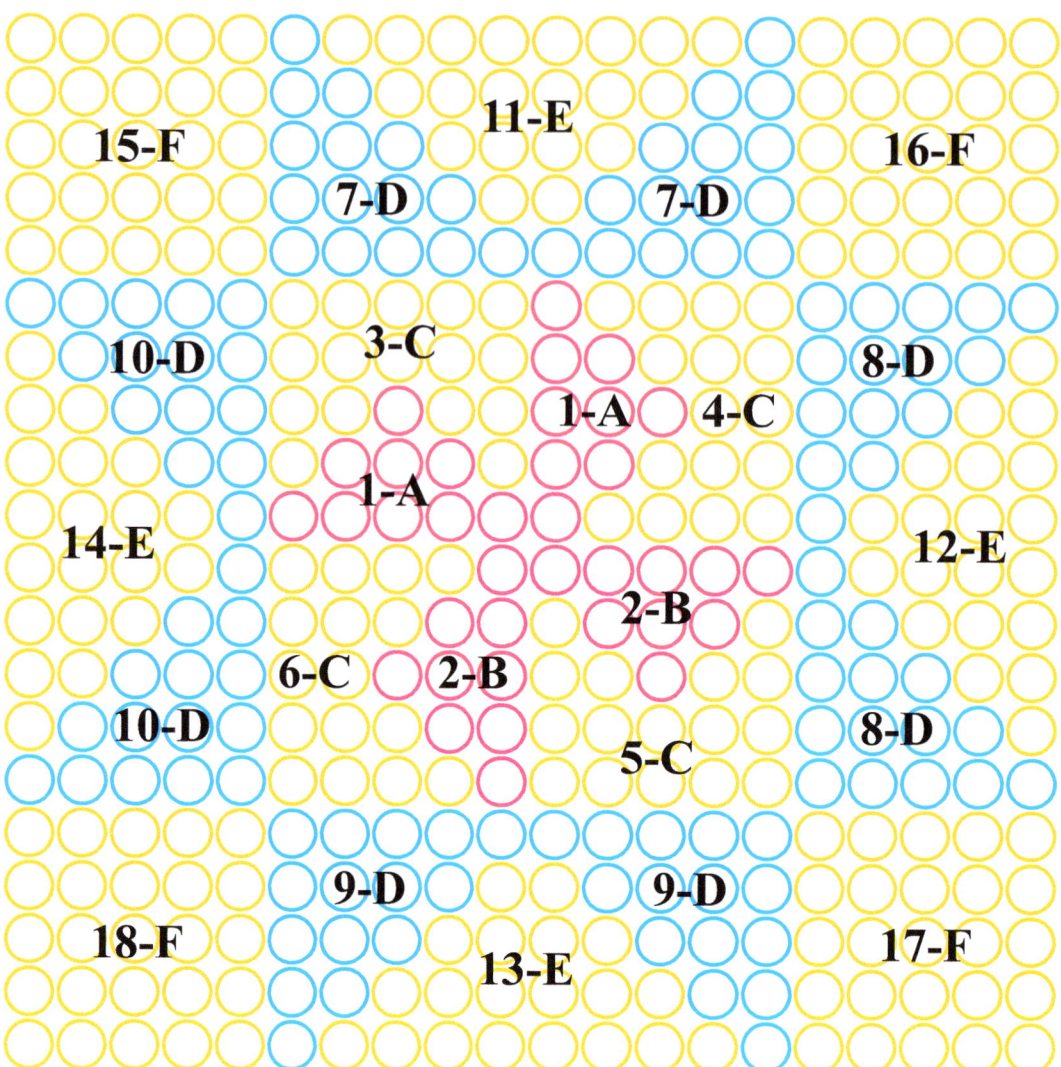

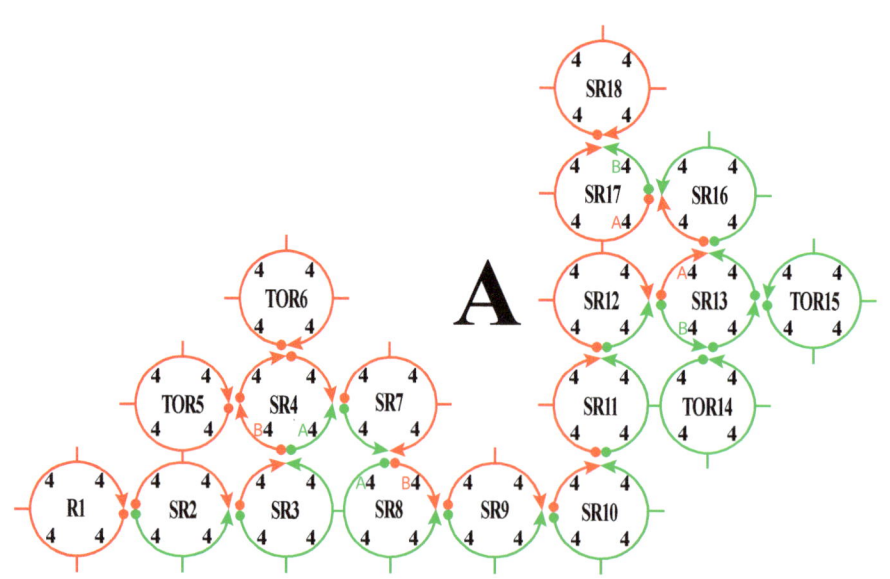

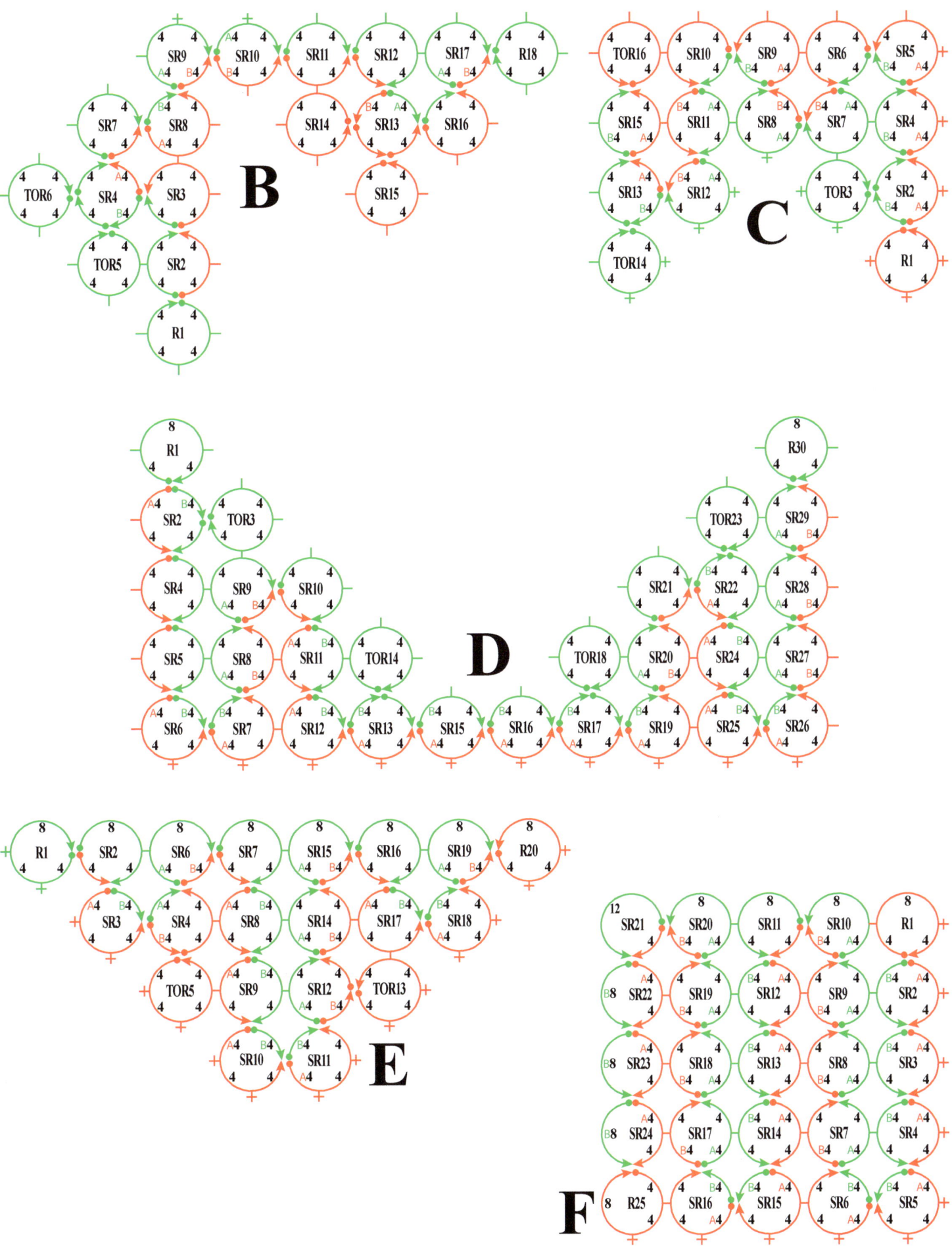

Broken Dishes #1

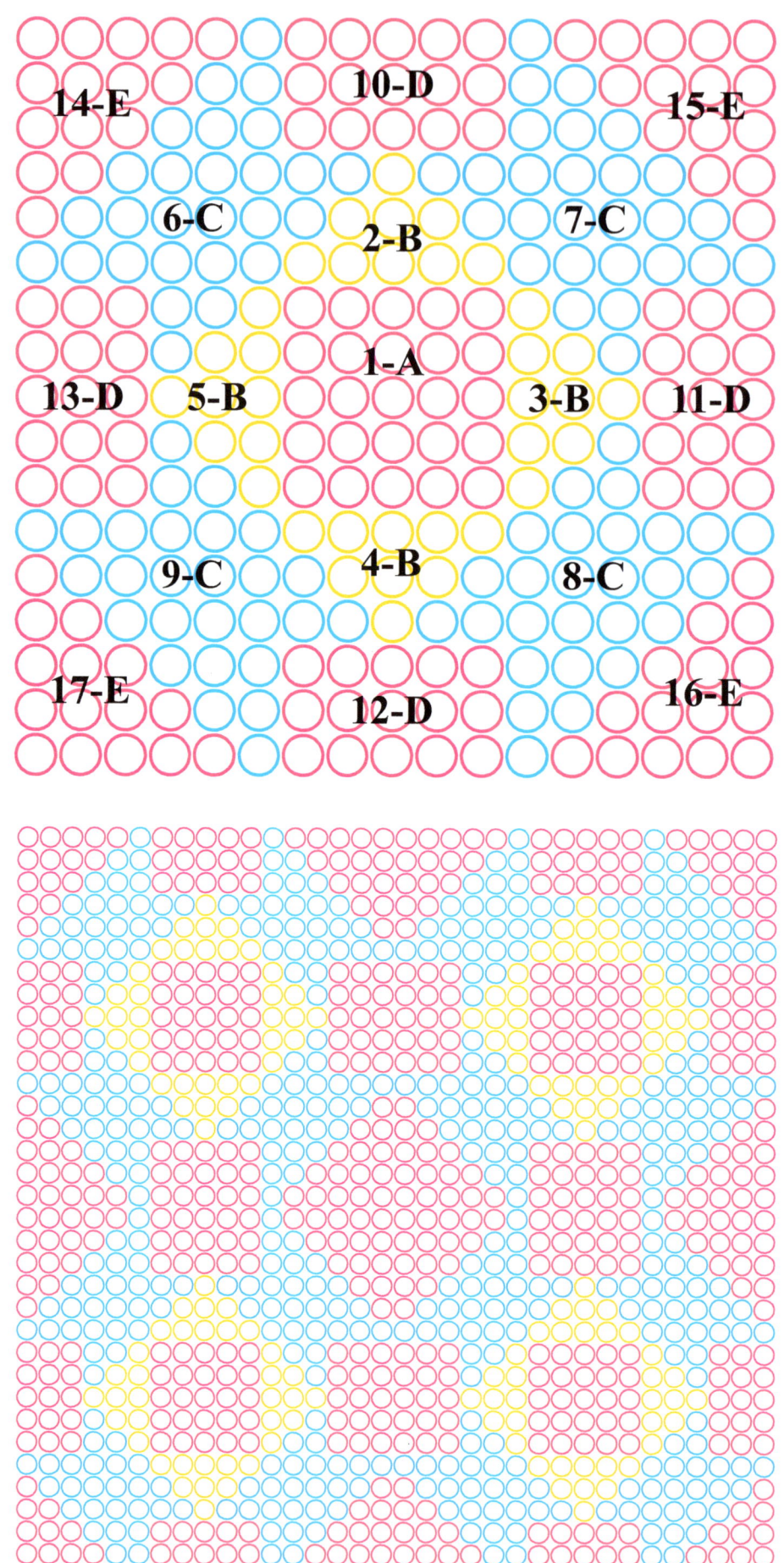

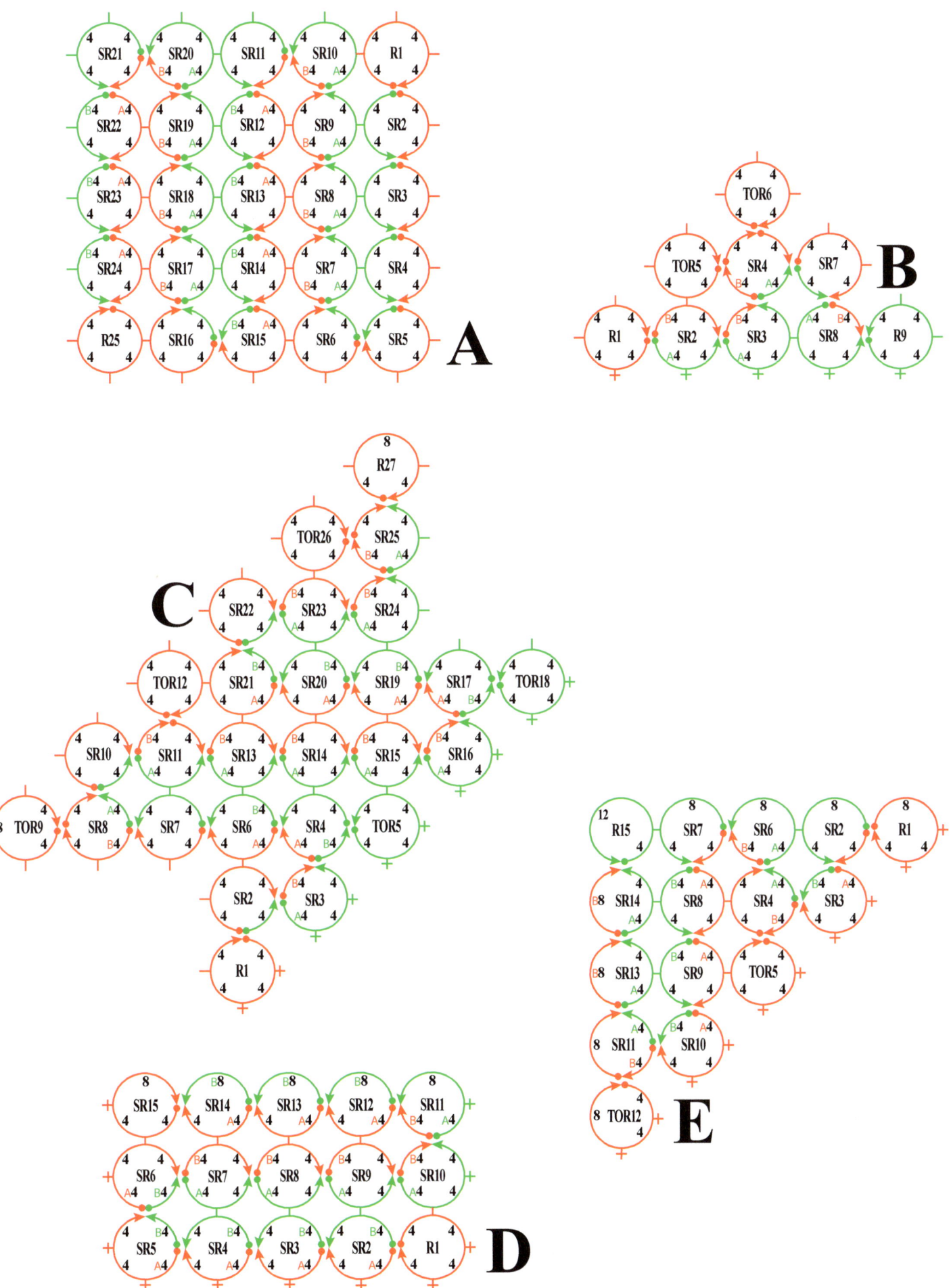

Solstice/Sawtooth Star

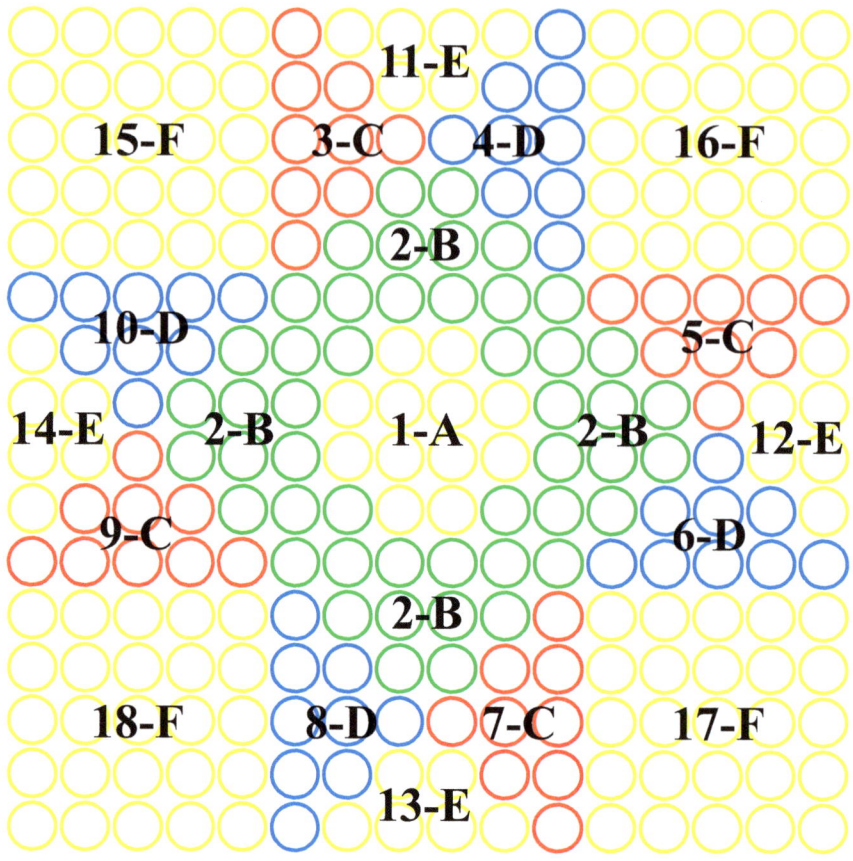

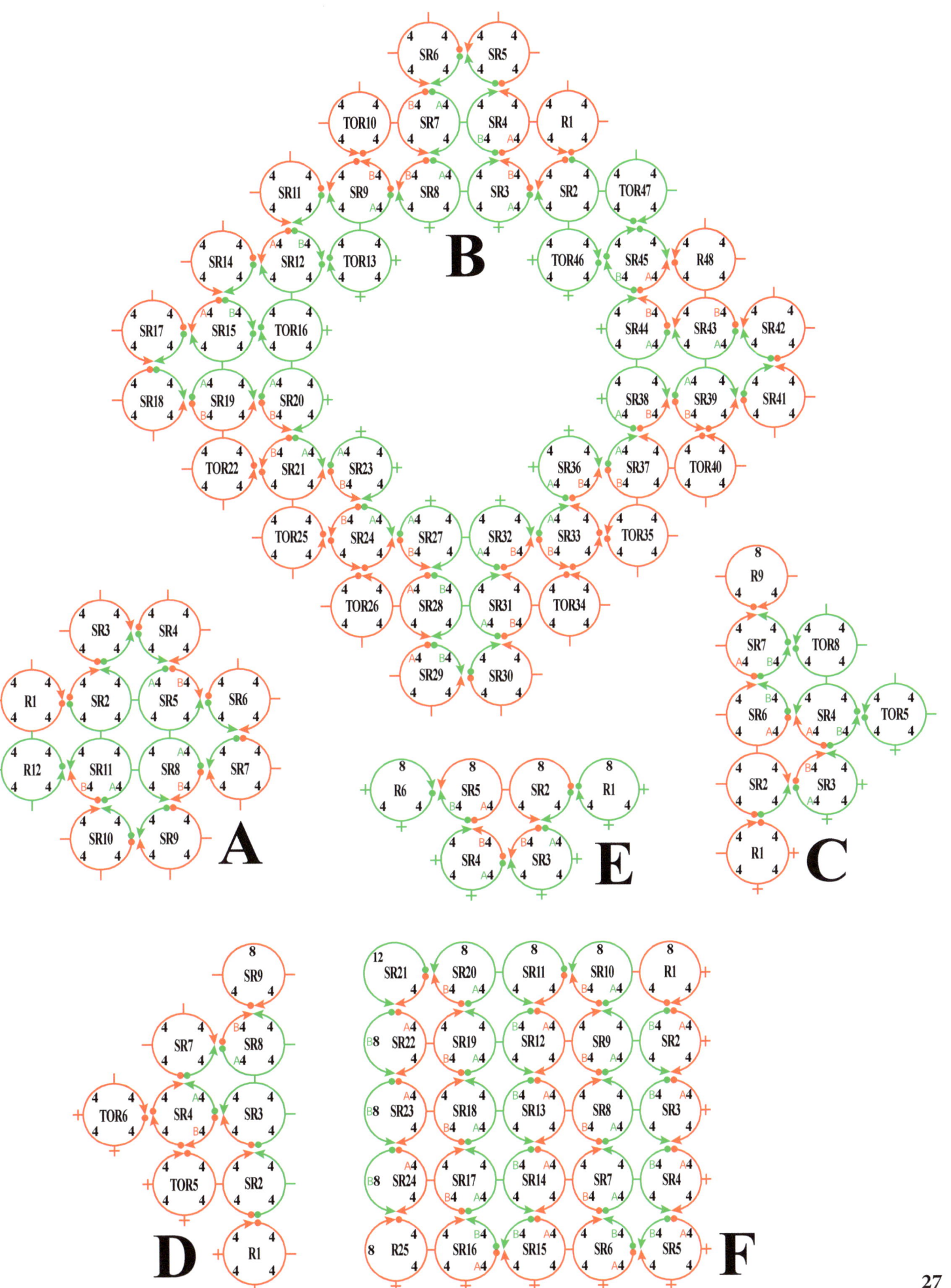

Perpetual Motion

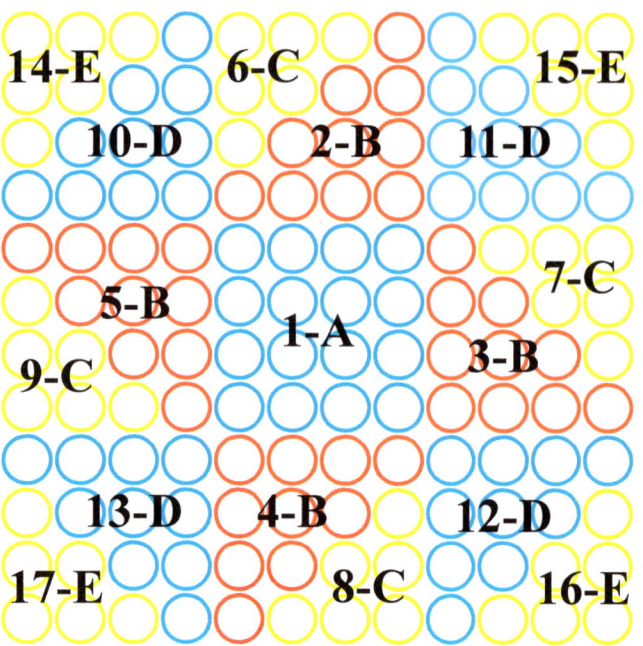

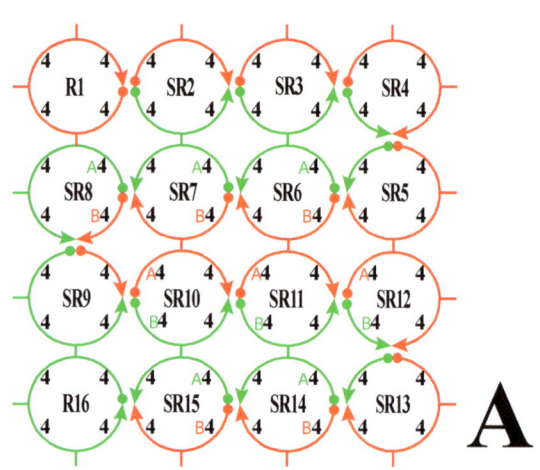
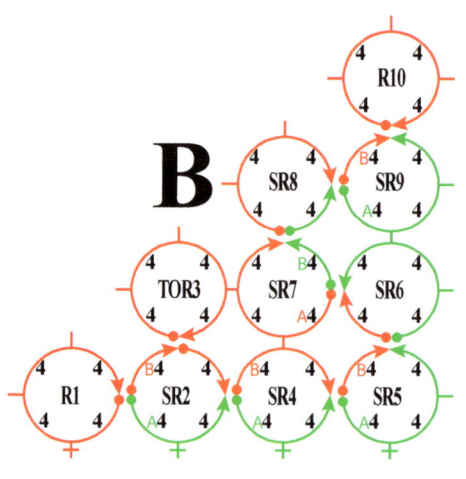

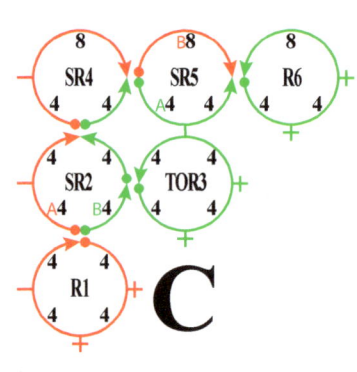
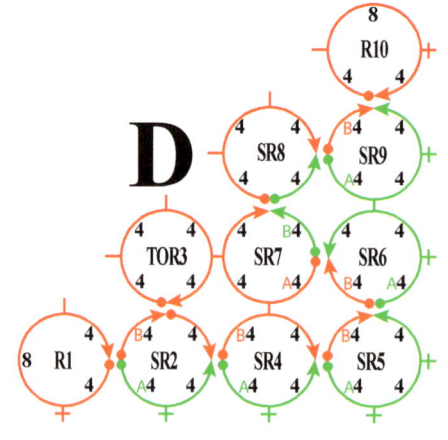
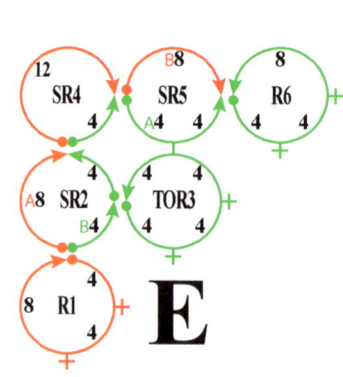

Farmers Daughter

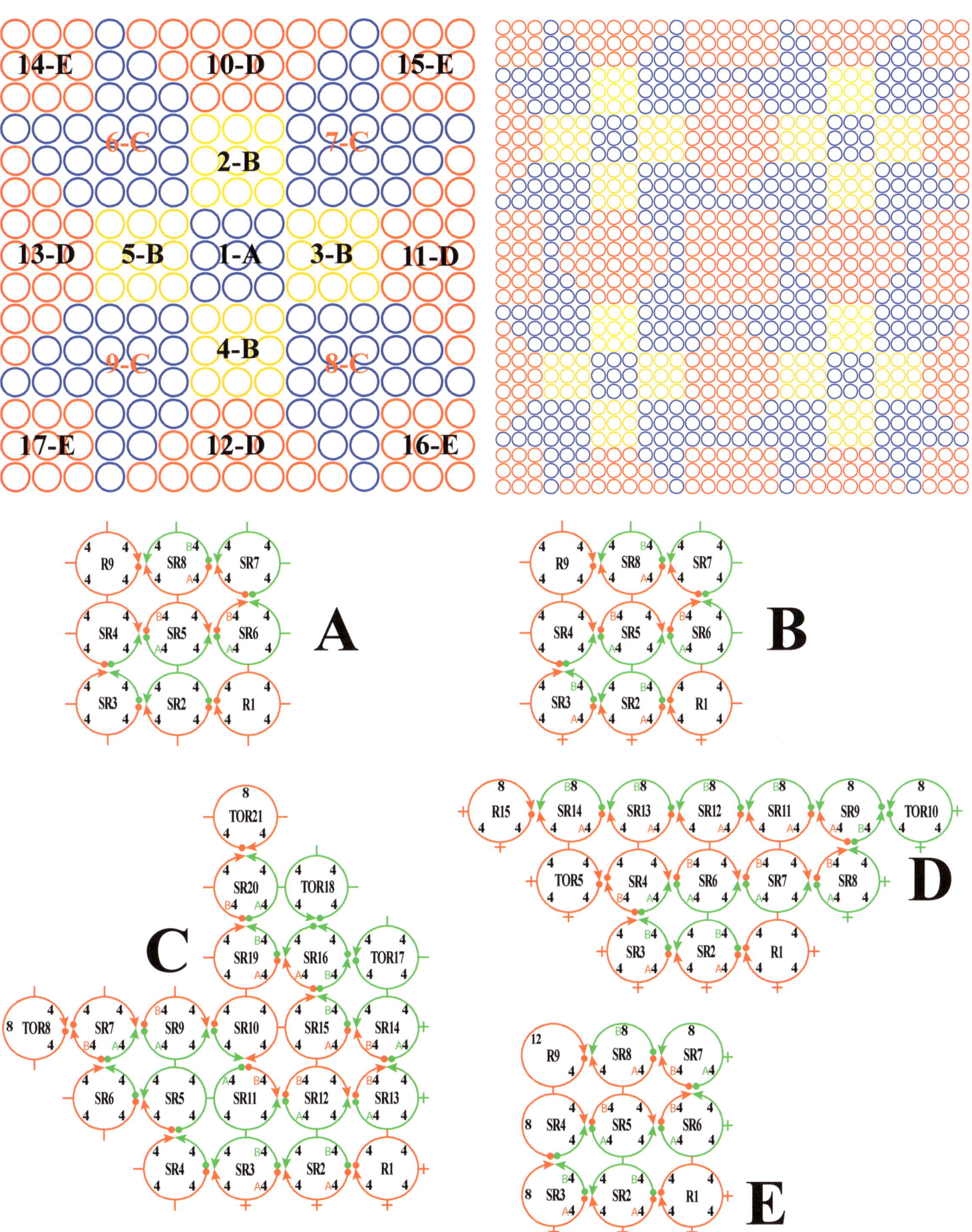

Beggar Block

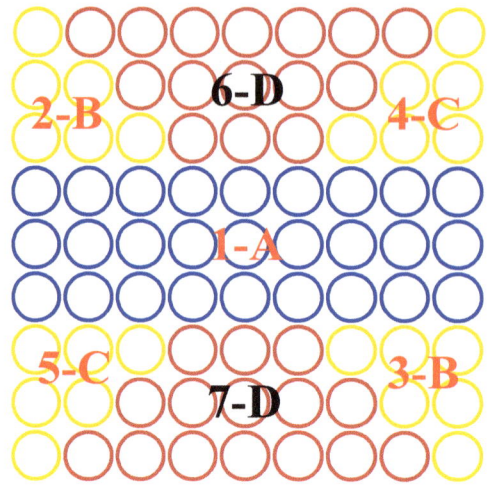

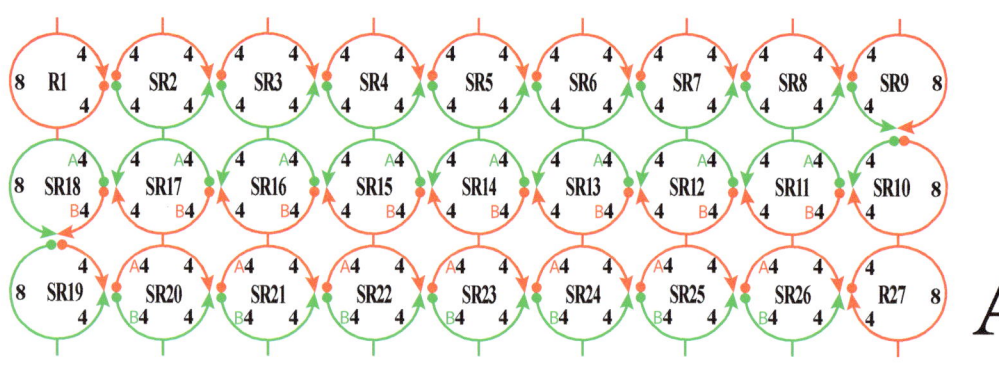
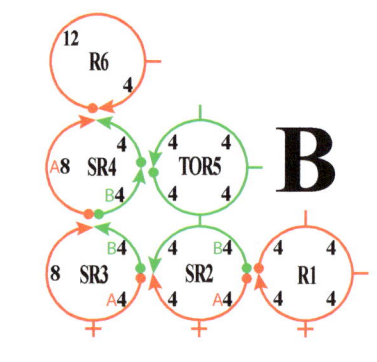

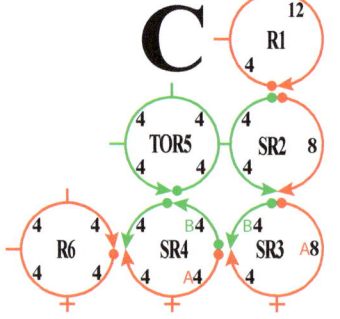
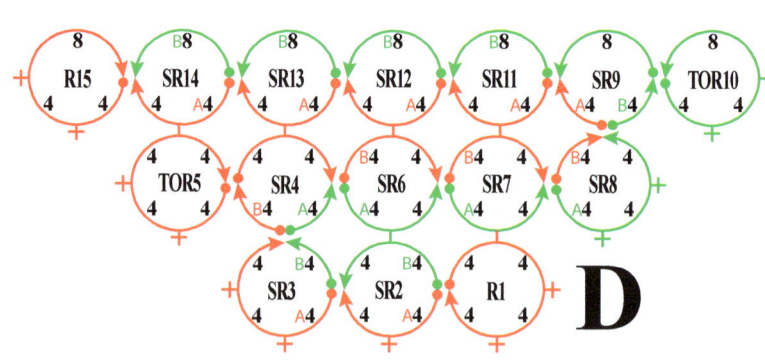

Disappearing 9 Patch

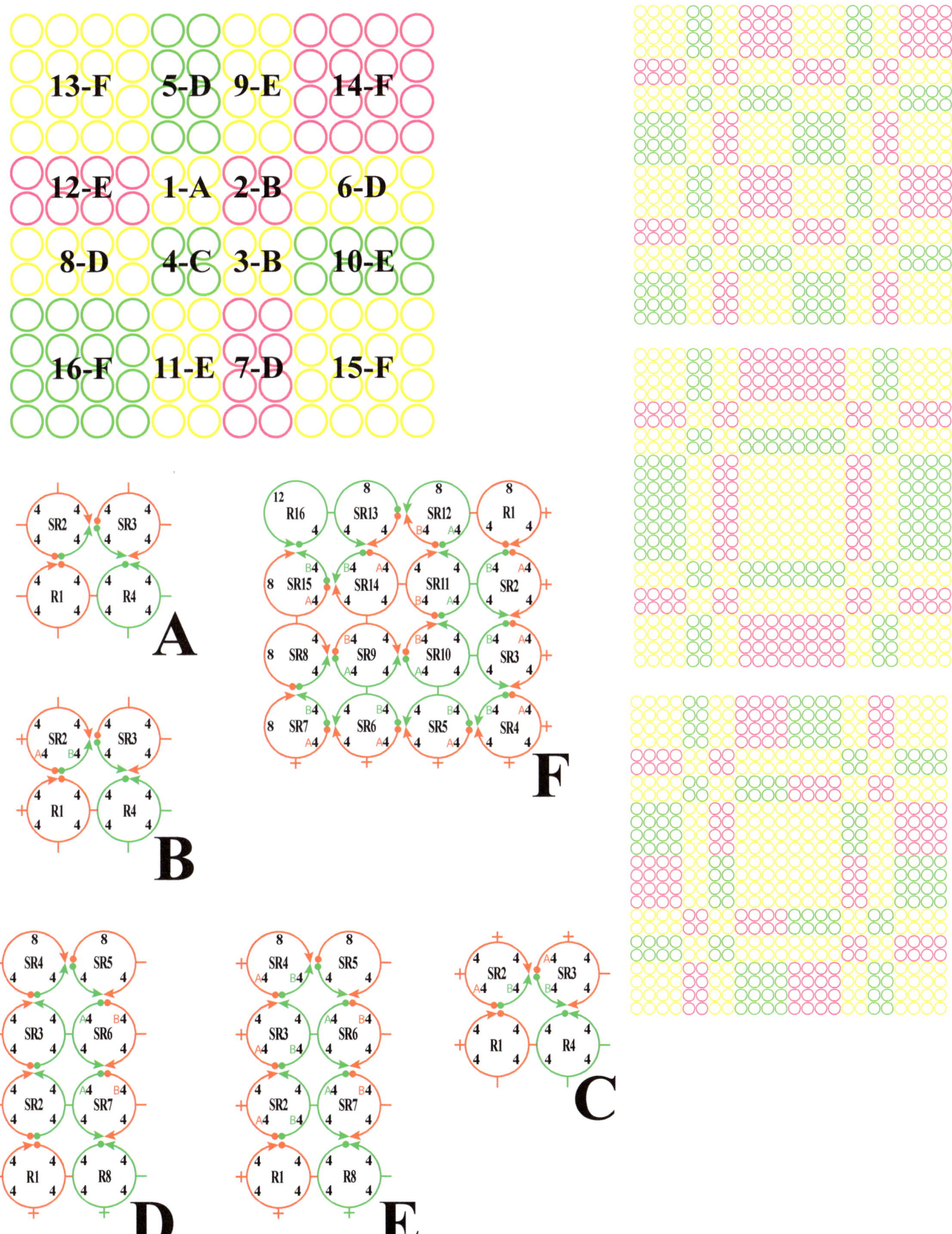

Wrench

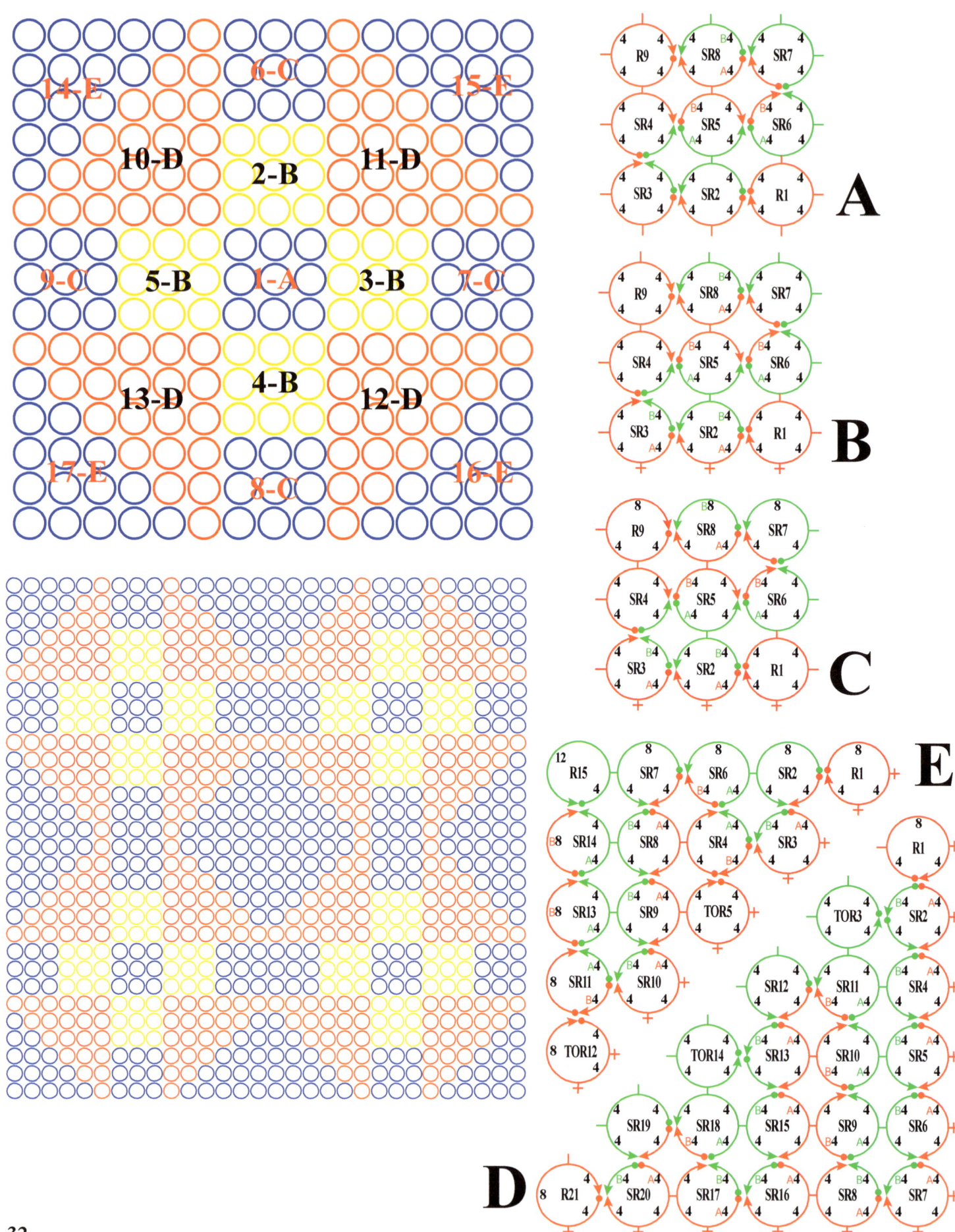

Broken Dishes #2

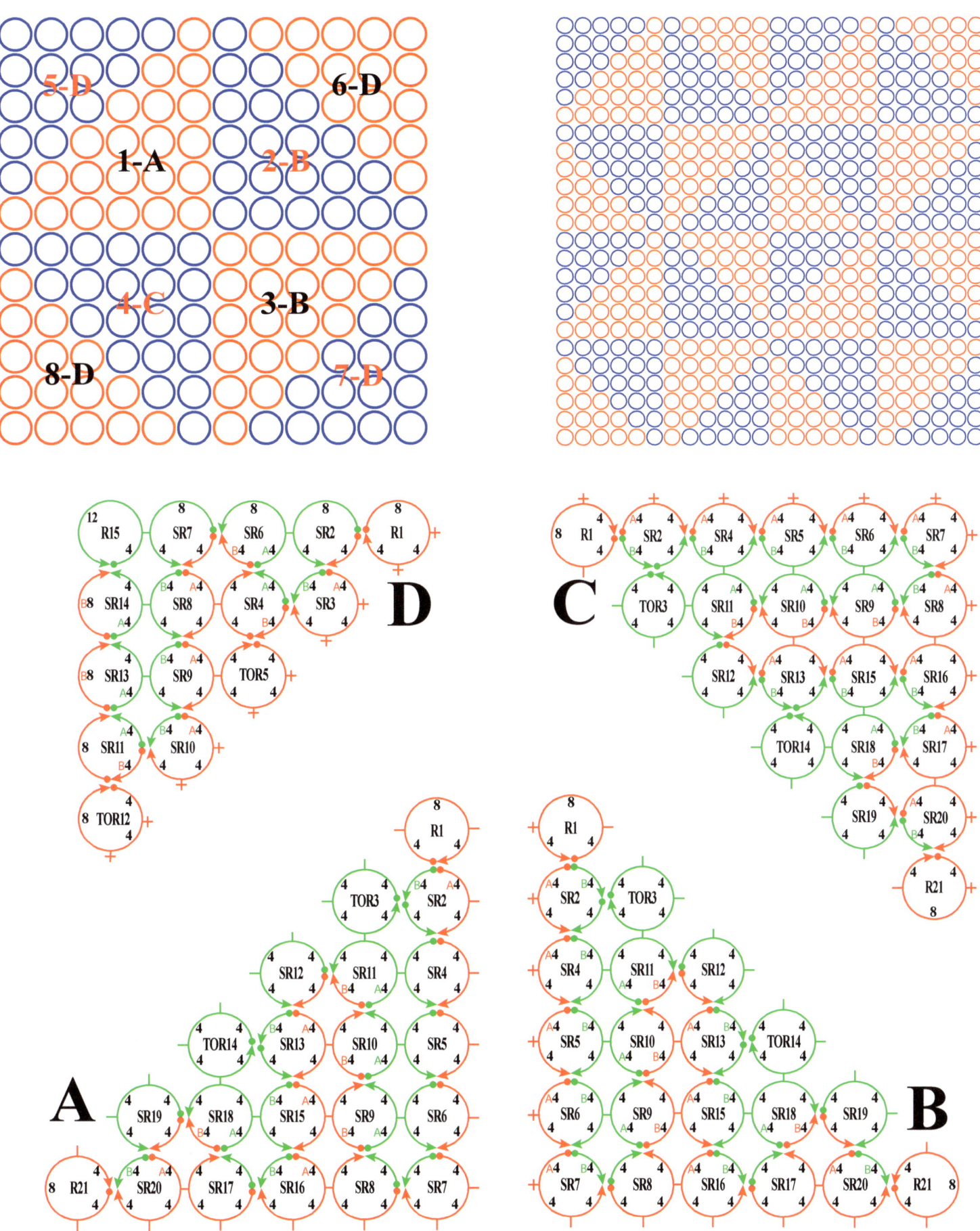

Bear Paw

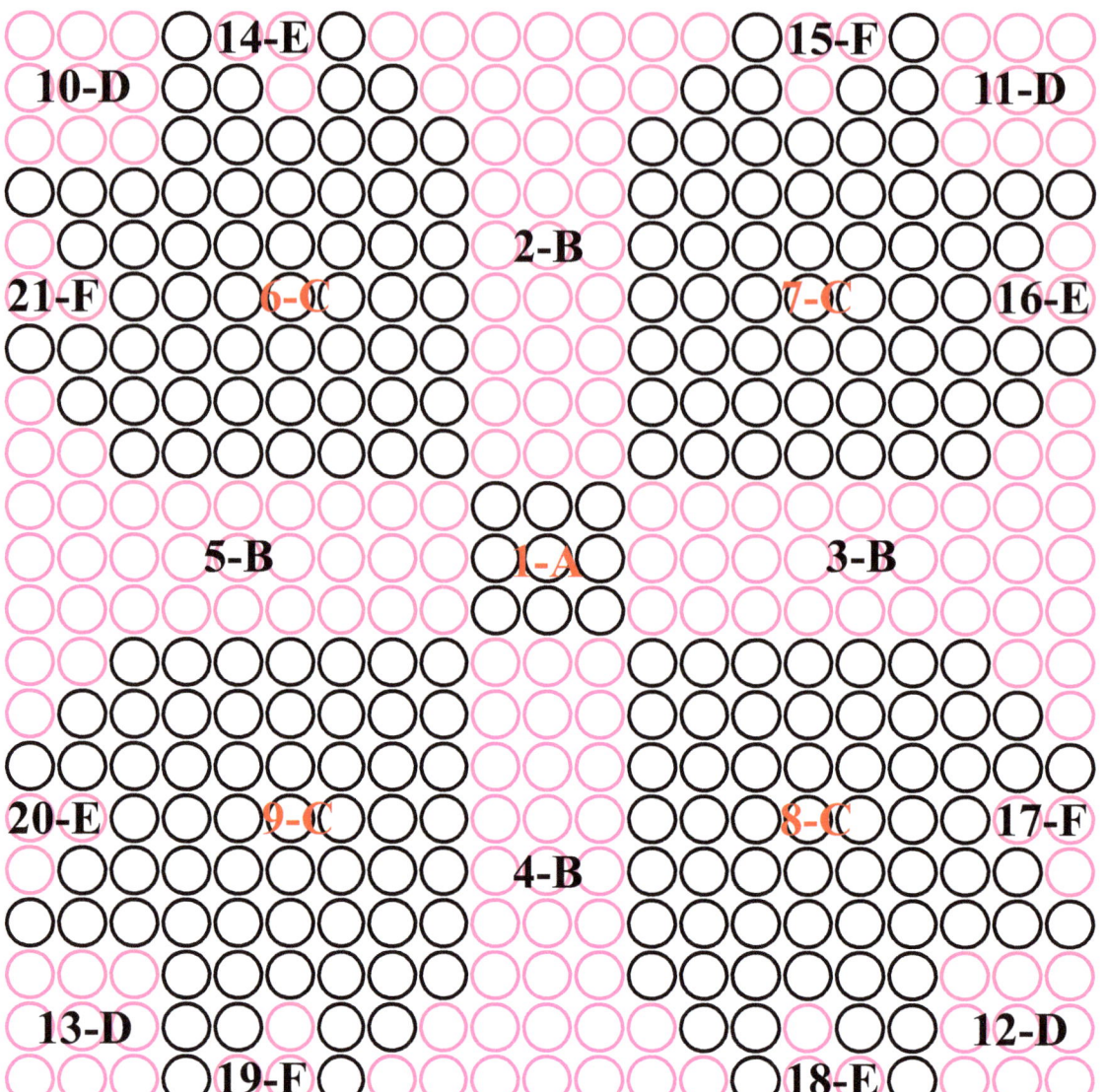

34

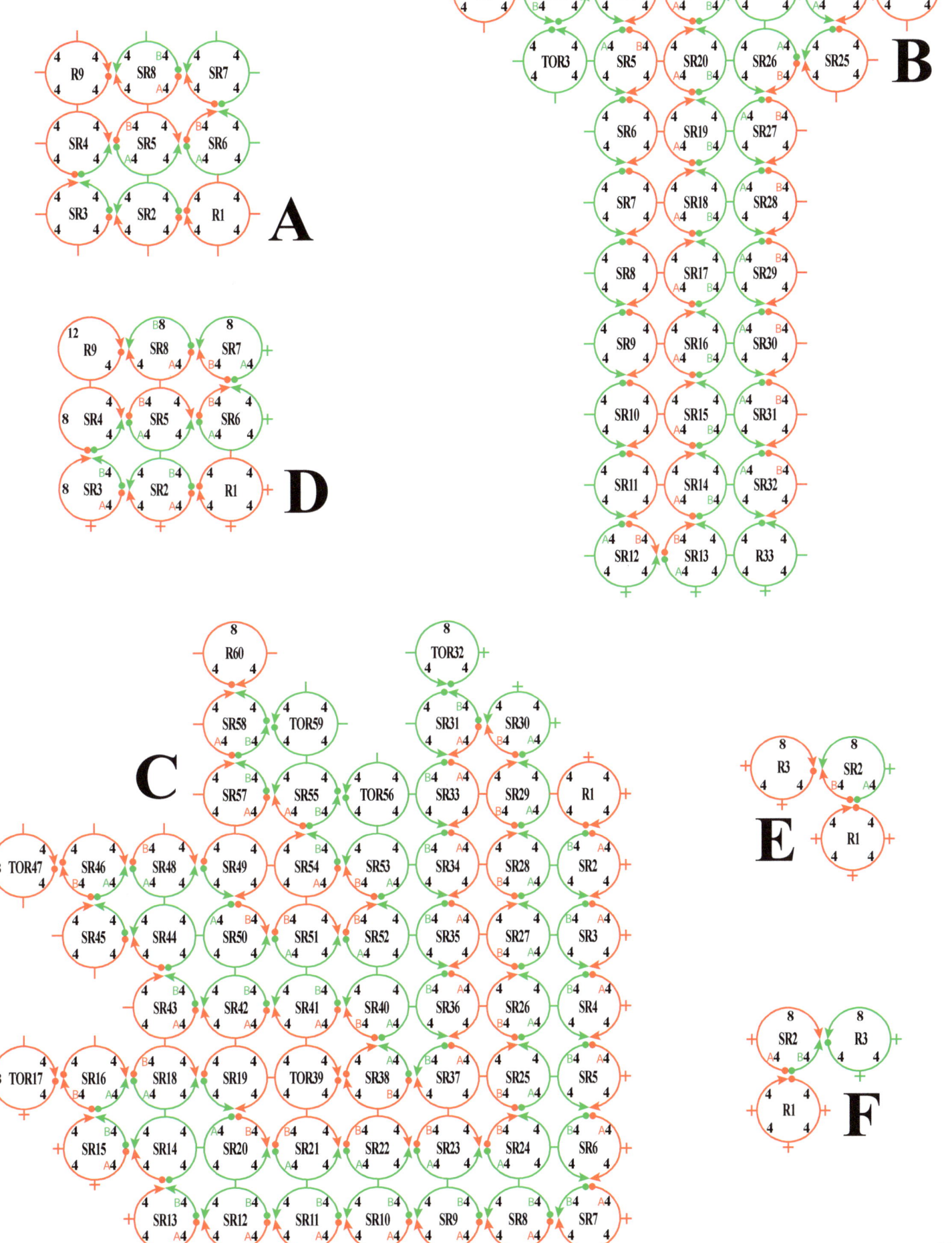

Sawtooth Star

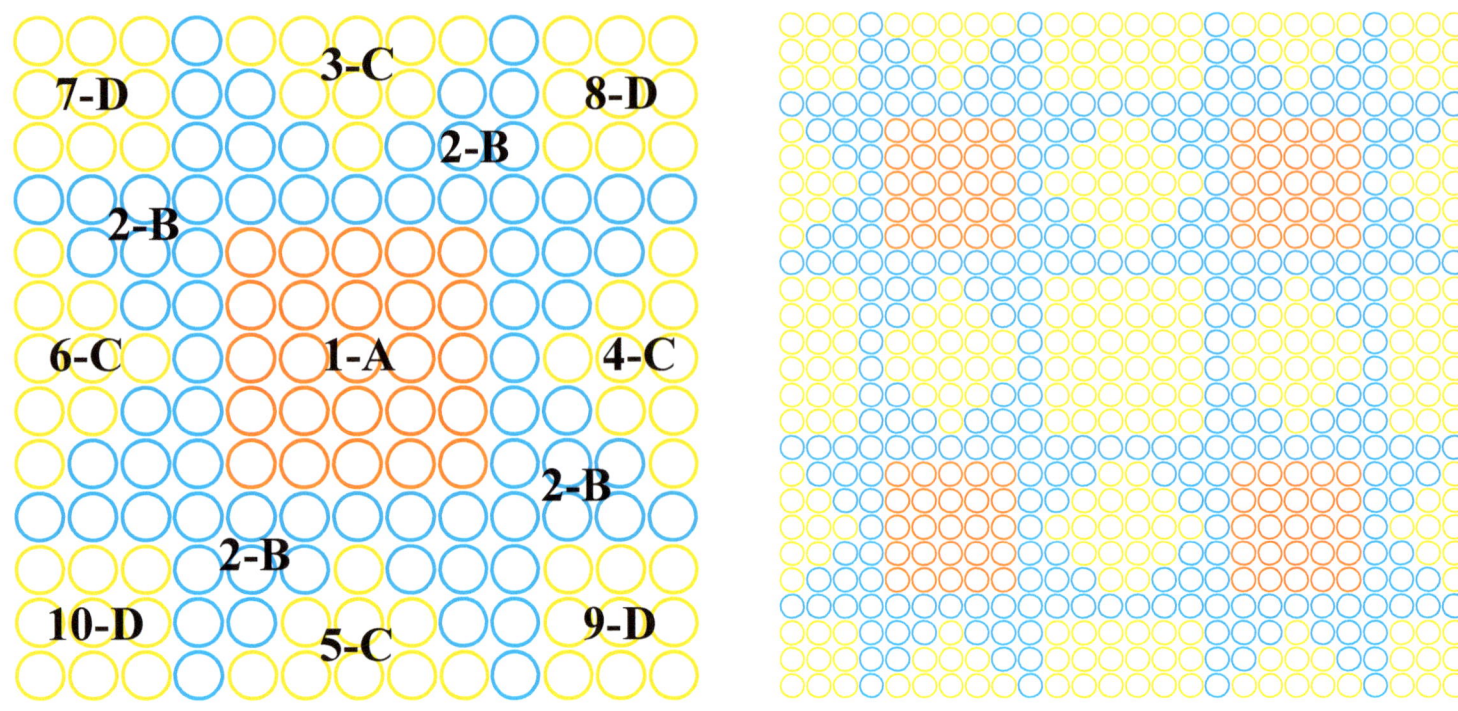

Alternative Way to Deal with Thread Ends--Mounting the Quilt Block to Fabric

I understand the big objection to working the Quilt-Inspired Split Ring Tatting designs is *"What about all those ends?!?!"* Playing with COLOR & SYMMETRY does come at a price---thread ends to finish! Because I use strategies to not have starting thread ends, I only have 2 thread ends per block piece to finish, those being the end threads. But even 'only' having 2 thread ends to finish can be a big deal when some of these patterns have up to 25-29 individual pieces in one patchwork block.

Finishing techniques are largely a matter of personal preference. I grew up sewing and doing other needlework so using a needle to 'sew-in' the thread ends into the rings seems perfectly natural/comfortable. I know many people who think using 'magic threads/loopers' is the only way to go. Good for them...but that technique is not for me.

So an alternative way to deal with thread ends is to pull them to the back of a piece of fabric.

I chose a piece of the tightest-woven, even-weave fabric that I had on hand (which is 28 count Quacker Cloth). Any tightly-woven fabric will do. The 'trick' is to choose a piece of fabric in which your thread ends (of various color saturations) will not show through to the frontside.

Using a crochet hook, pull the thread ends through to the backside of the fabric. I brought each of the 2 thread ends of one 'piece' through so that they were one or two fabric threads apart. Then I tied a square knot with these 2 thread ends, anchoring the work to the fabric base. I cut my ends, leaving sightly less than 1/4 inch threads ends as insurance that my square knot would not come undone.

If you need additional thread to sew down your work to the fabric *(such as using the piece on clothing, a quilt top, etc.)* separate the thread you used to tat the piece into the 2 or 3 plys of thread from one another. Use one of the plys as your stitching thread. It will show on the back, but matches your work on the front perfectly.

Frontside of work mounted to fabric

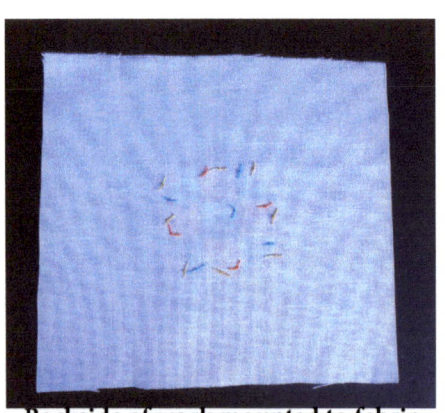
Backside of work mounted to fabric

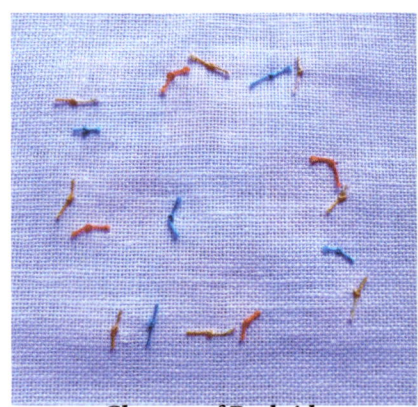
Closeup of Backside

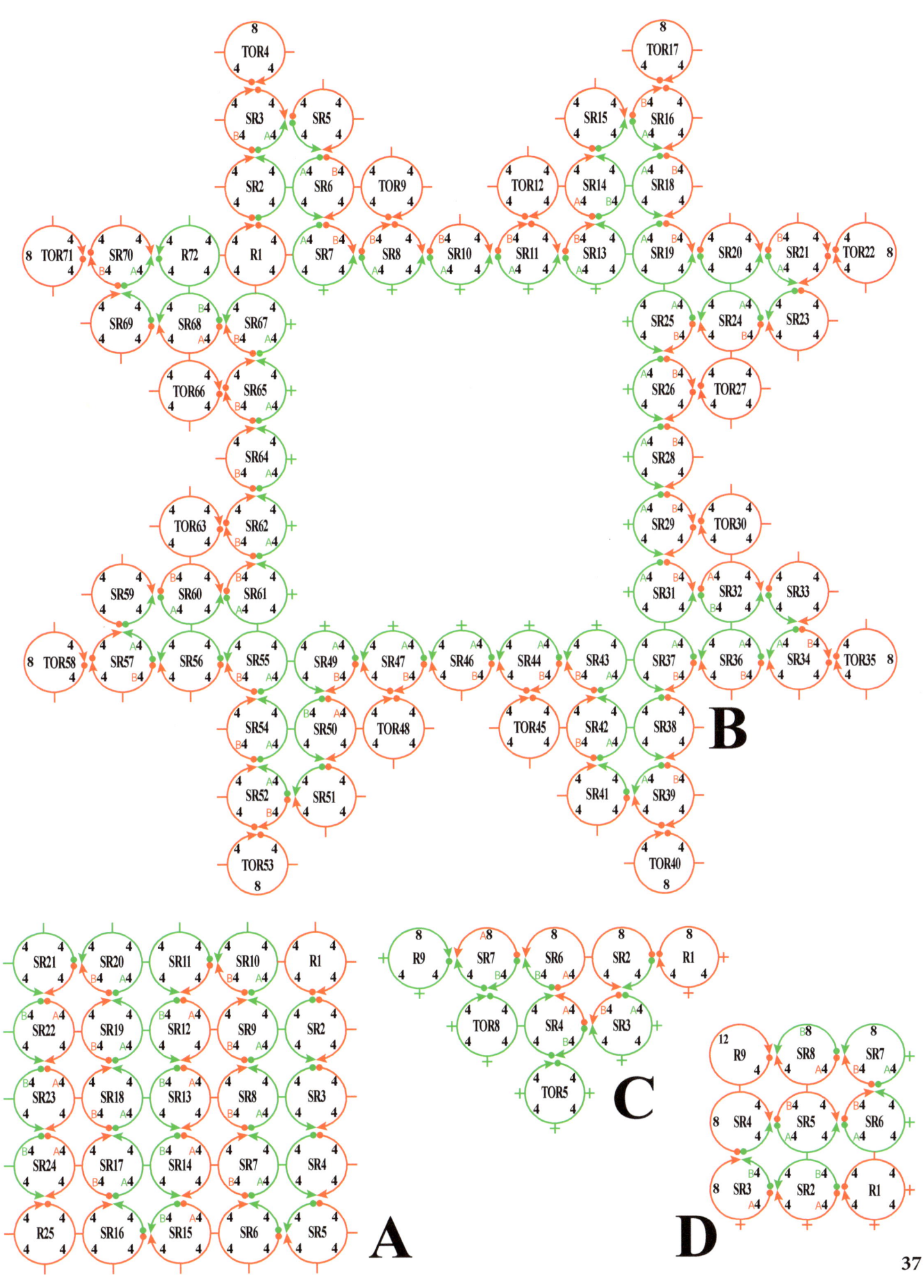

Hen & Chicks/Duck & Ducklings

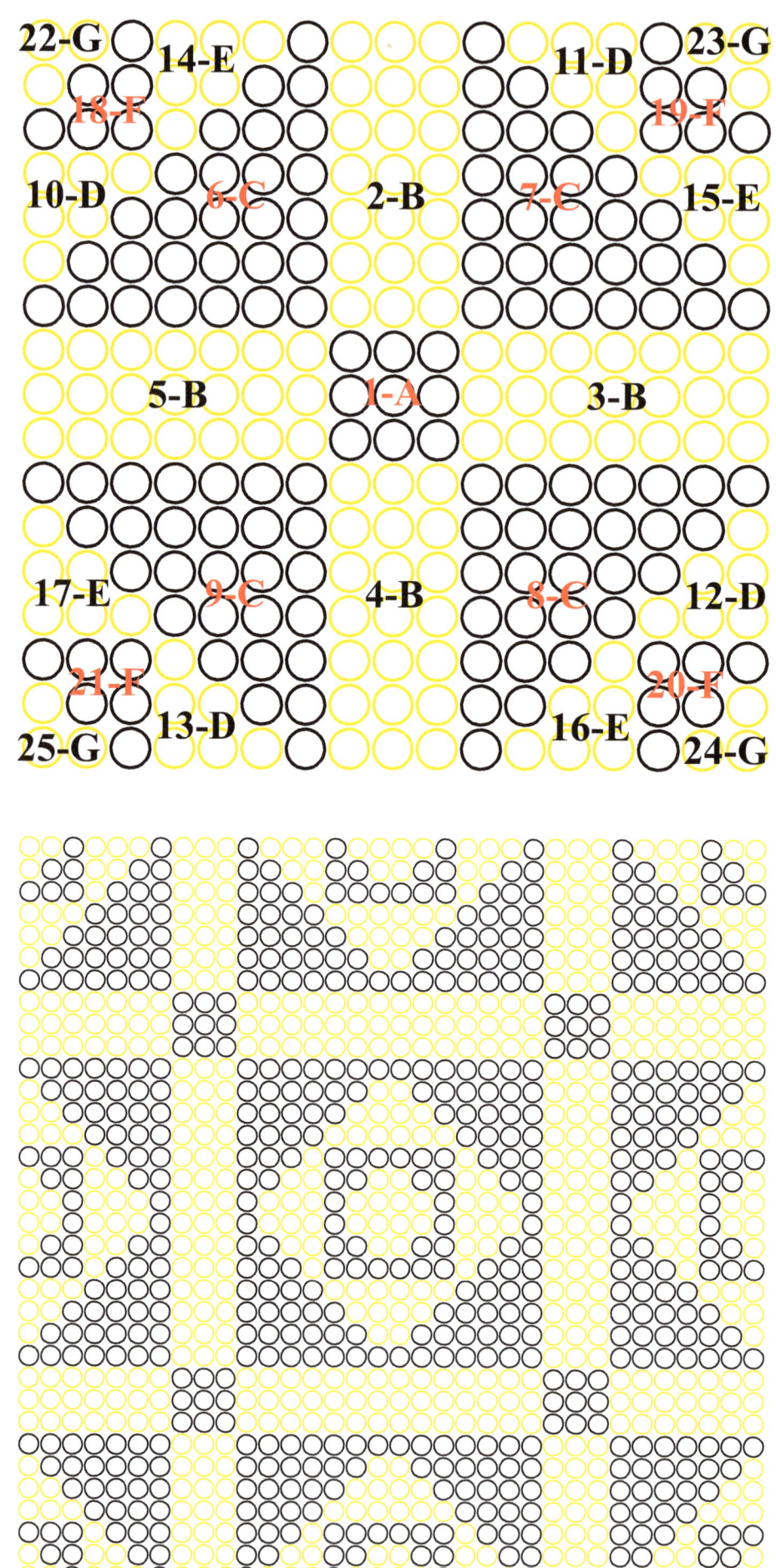

38

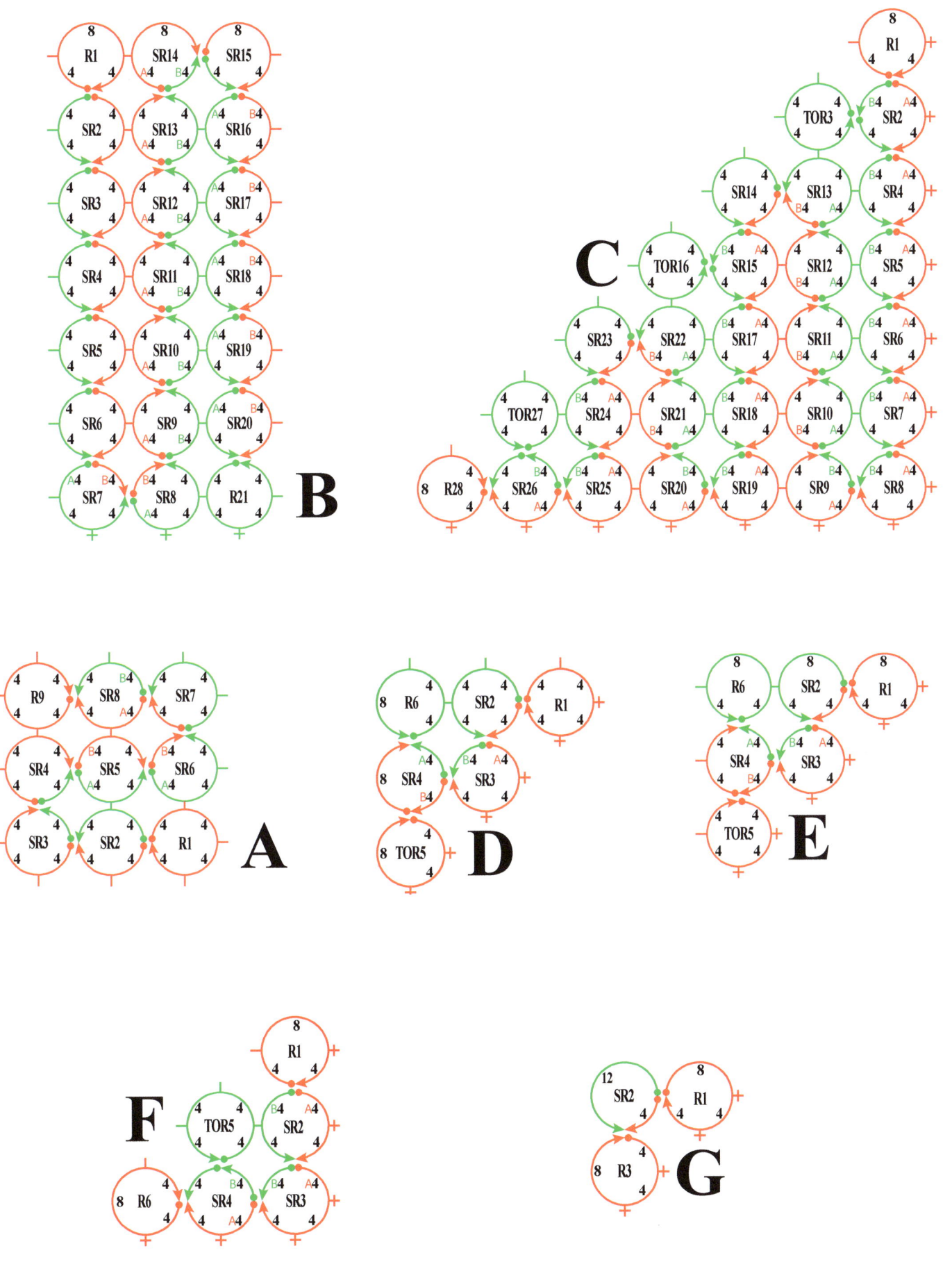

Jack in the Pulpit

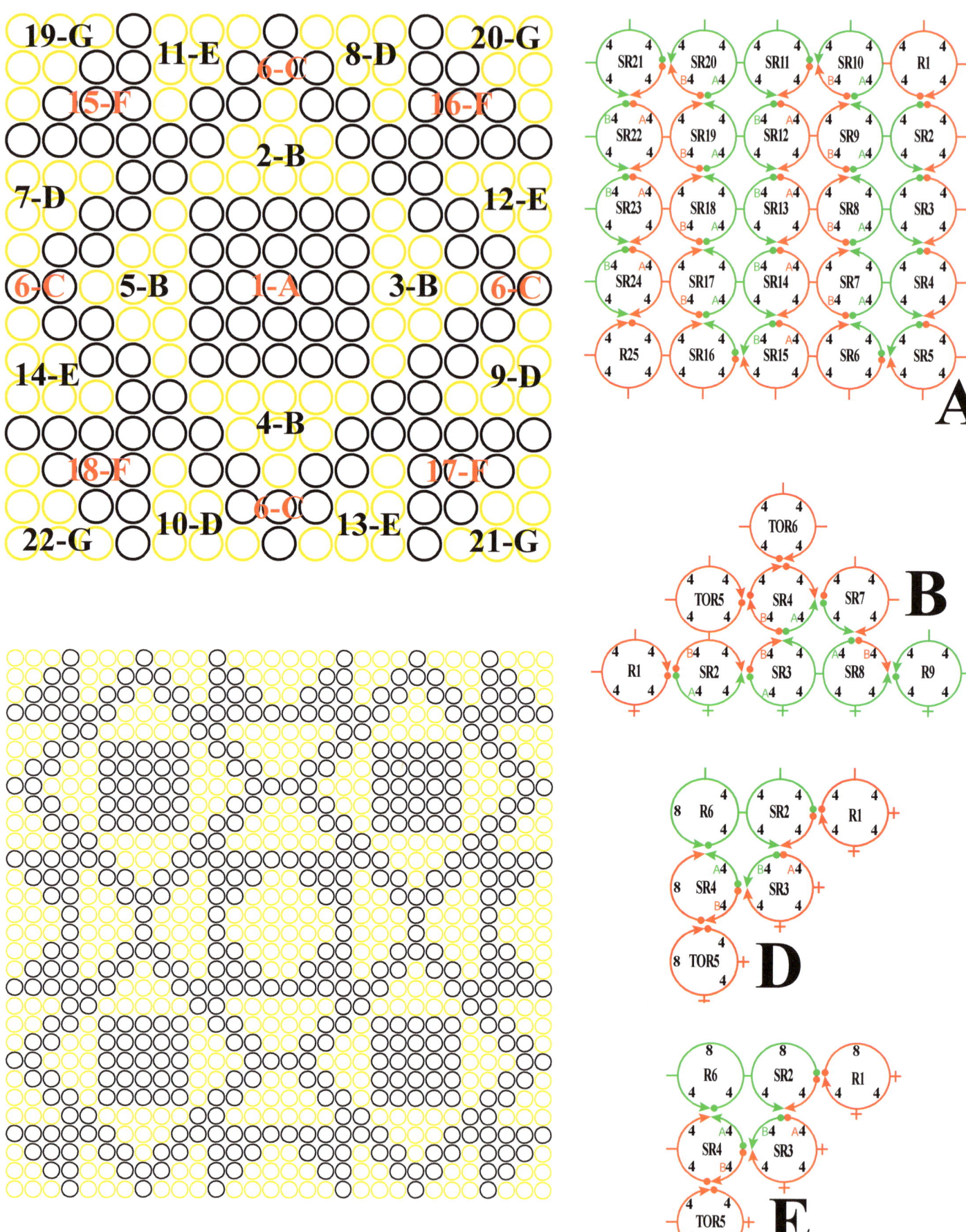

41

Whirlwind 1

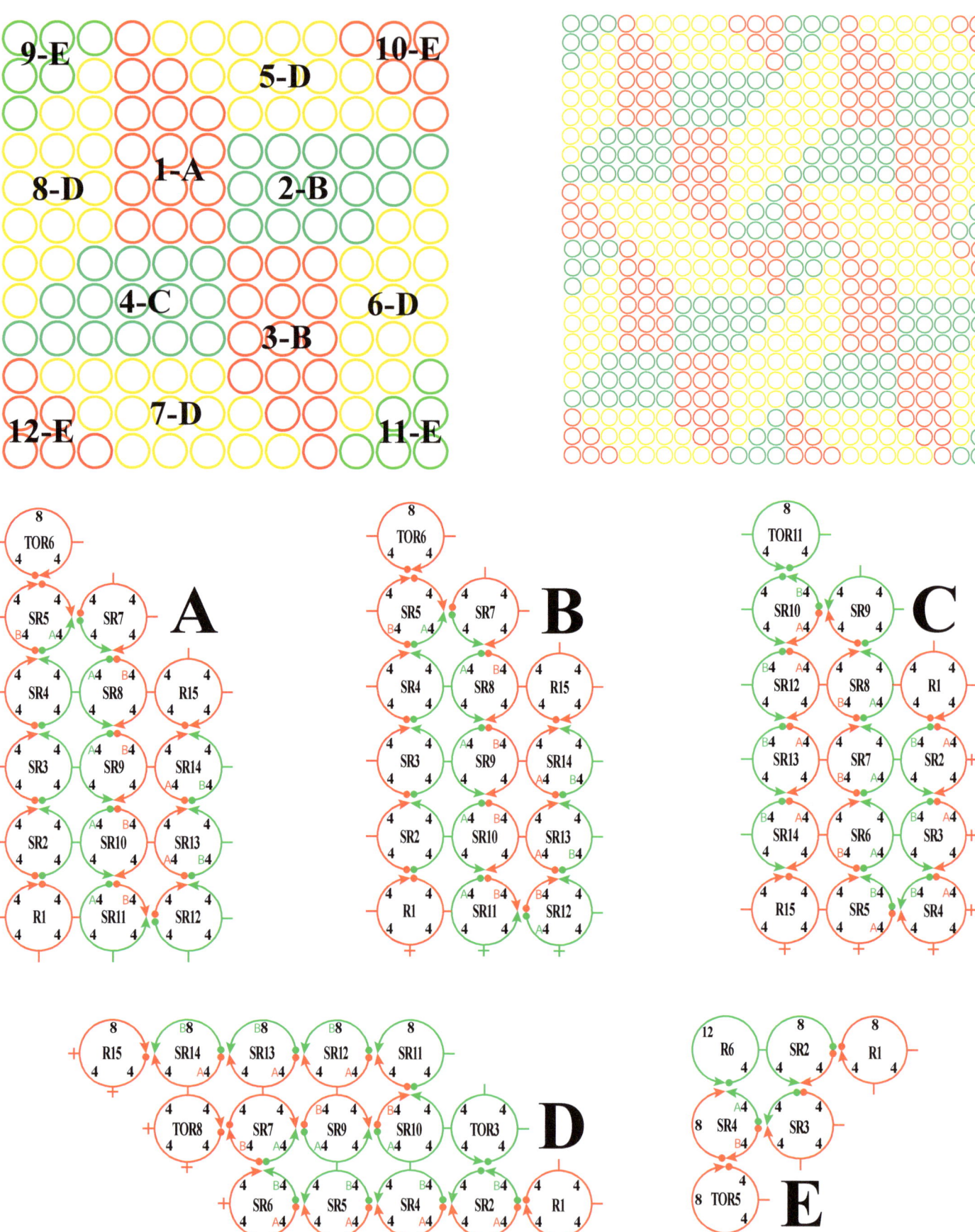

Whirlwind 2

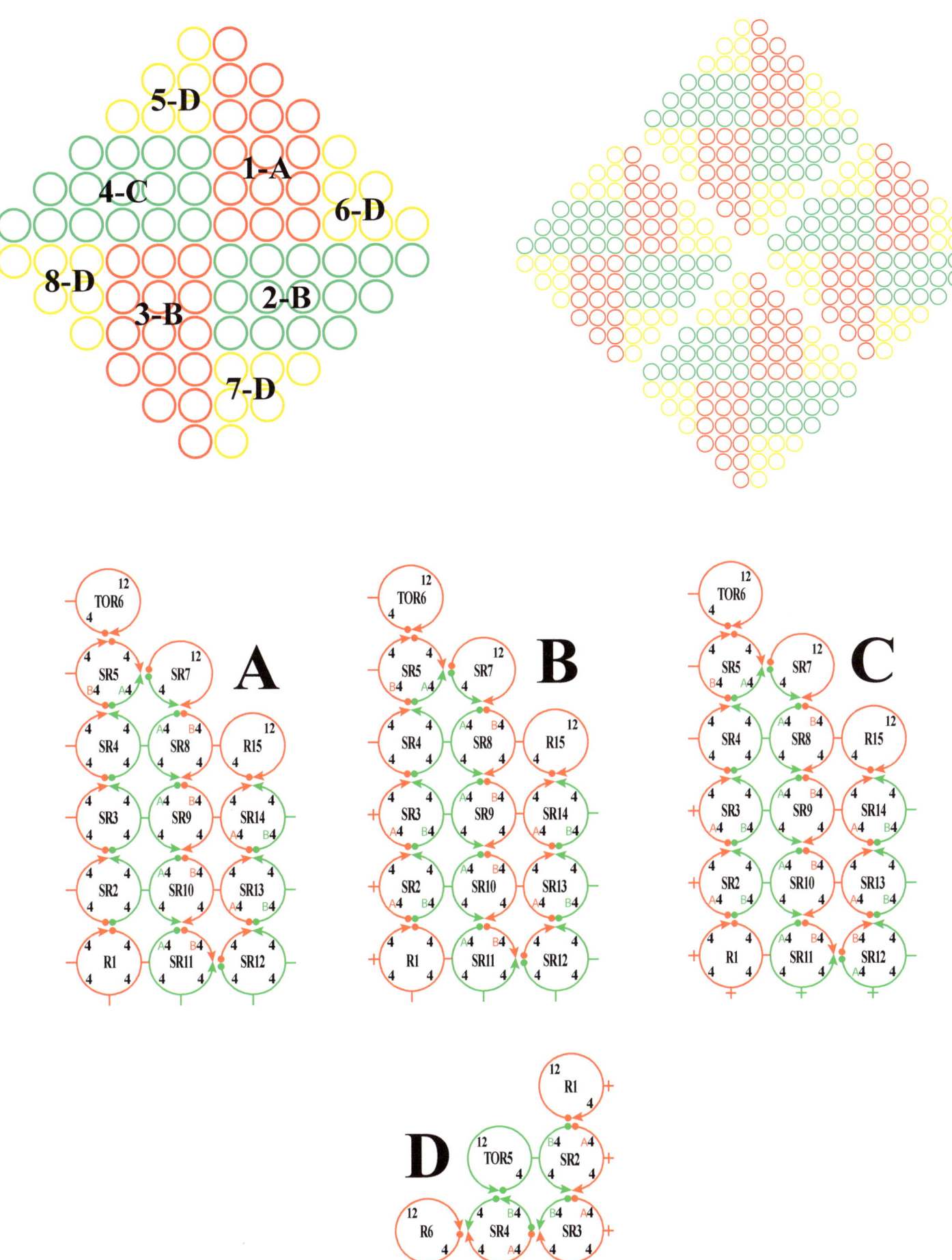

Weathervane

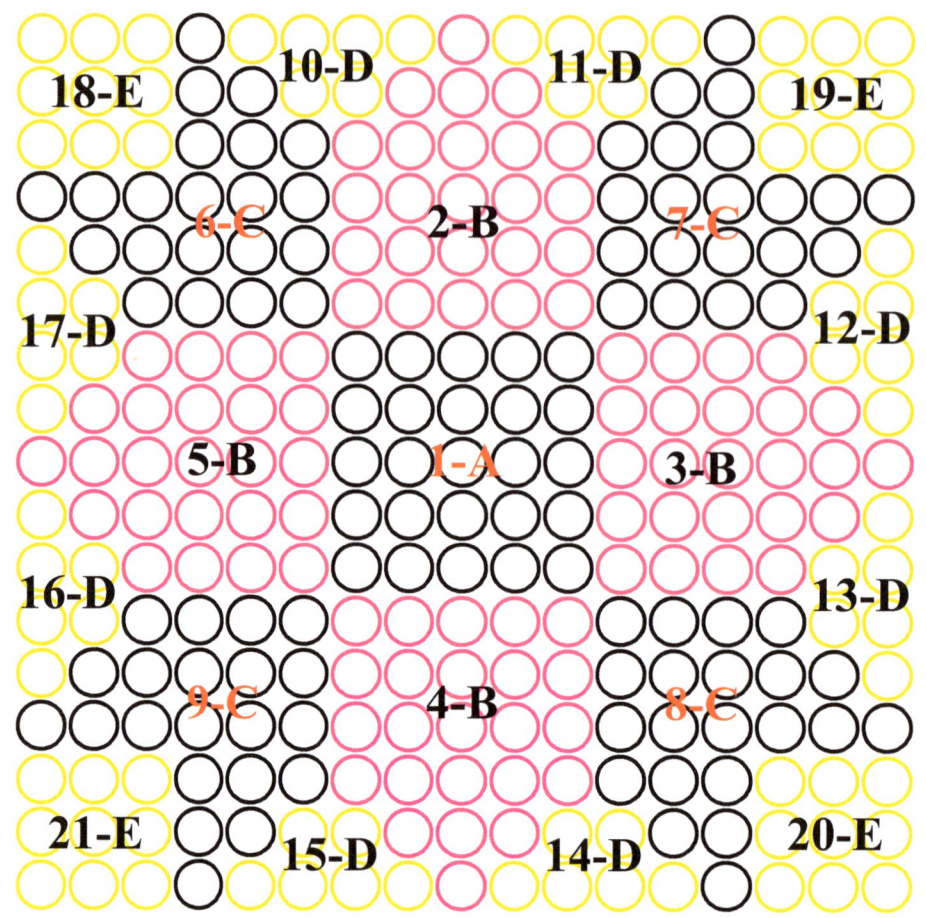

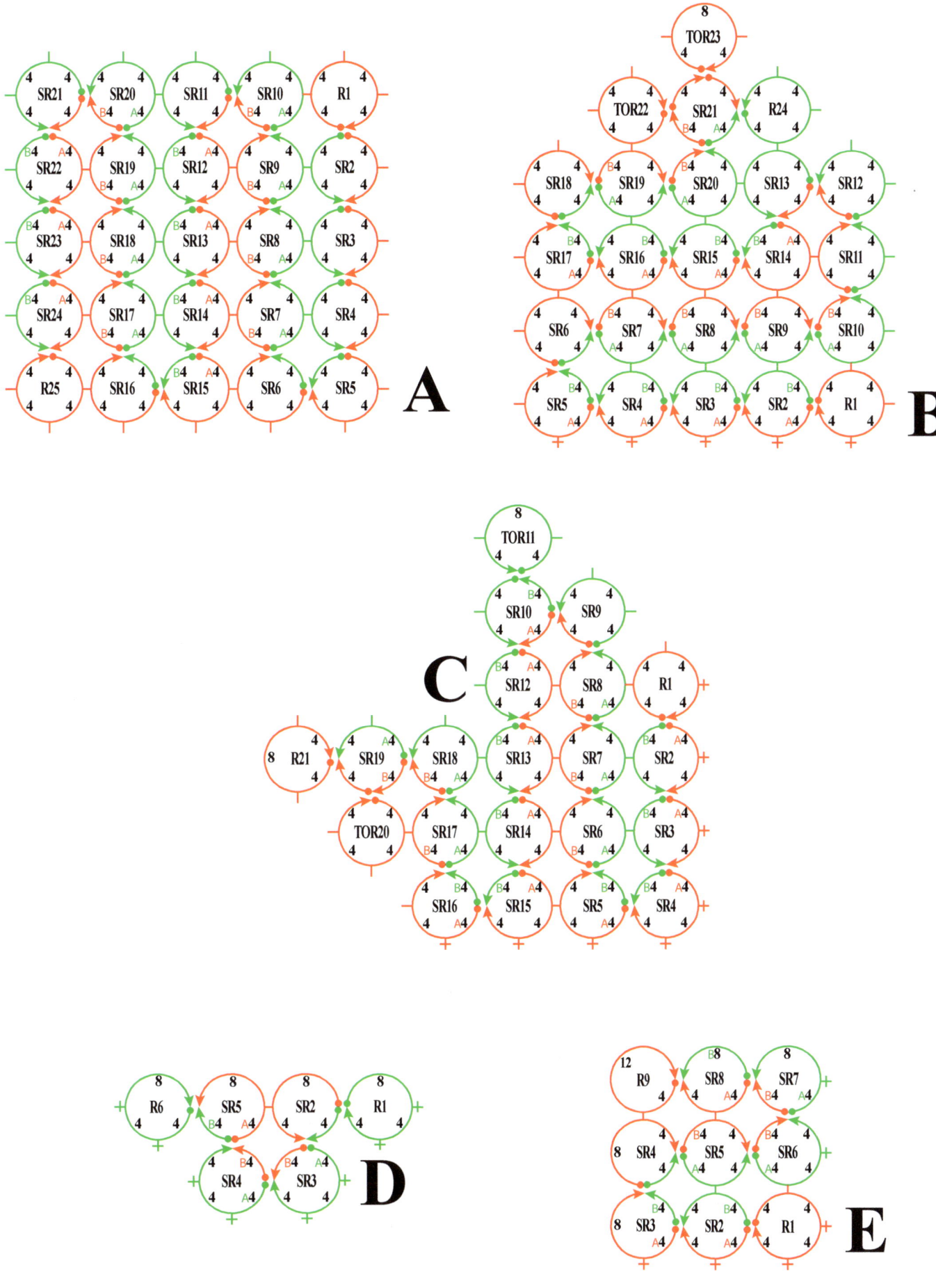

Cats Cradle

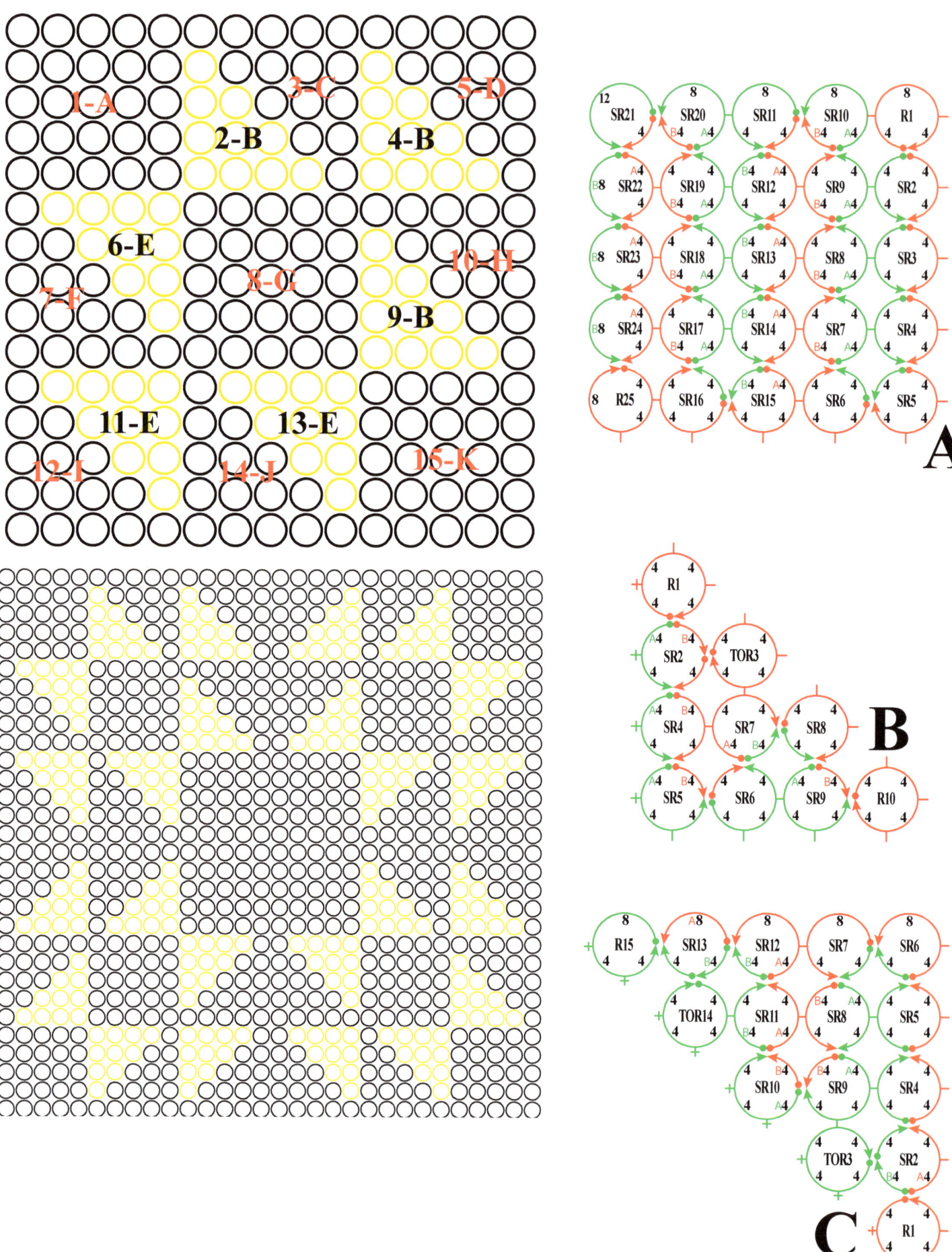

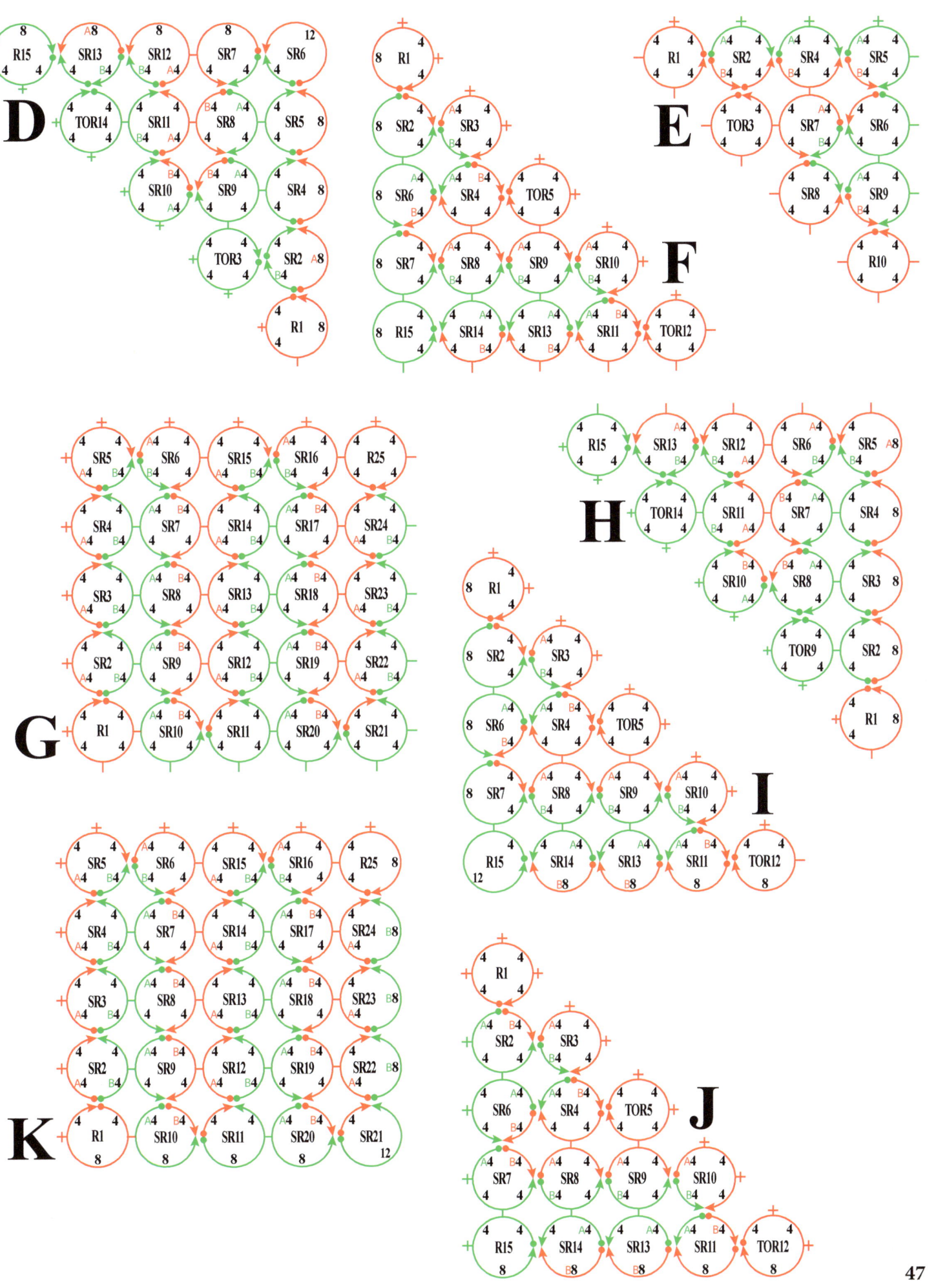

Bird in the Air

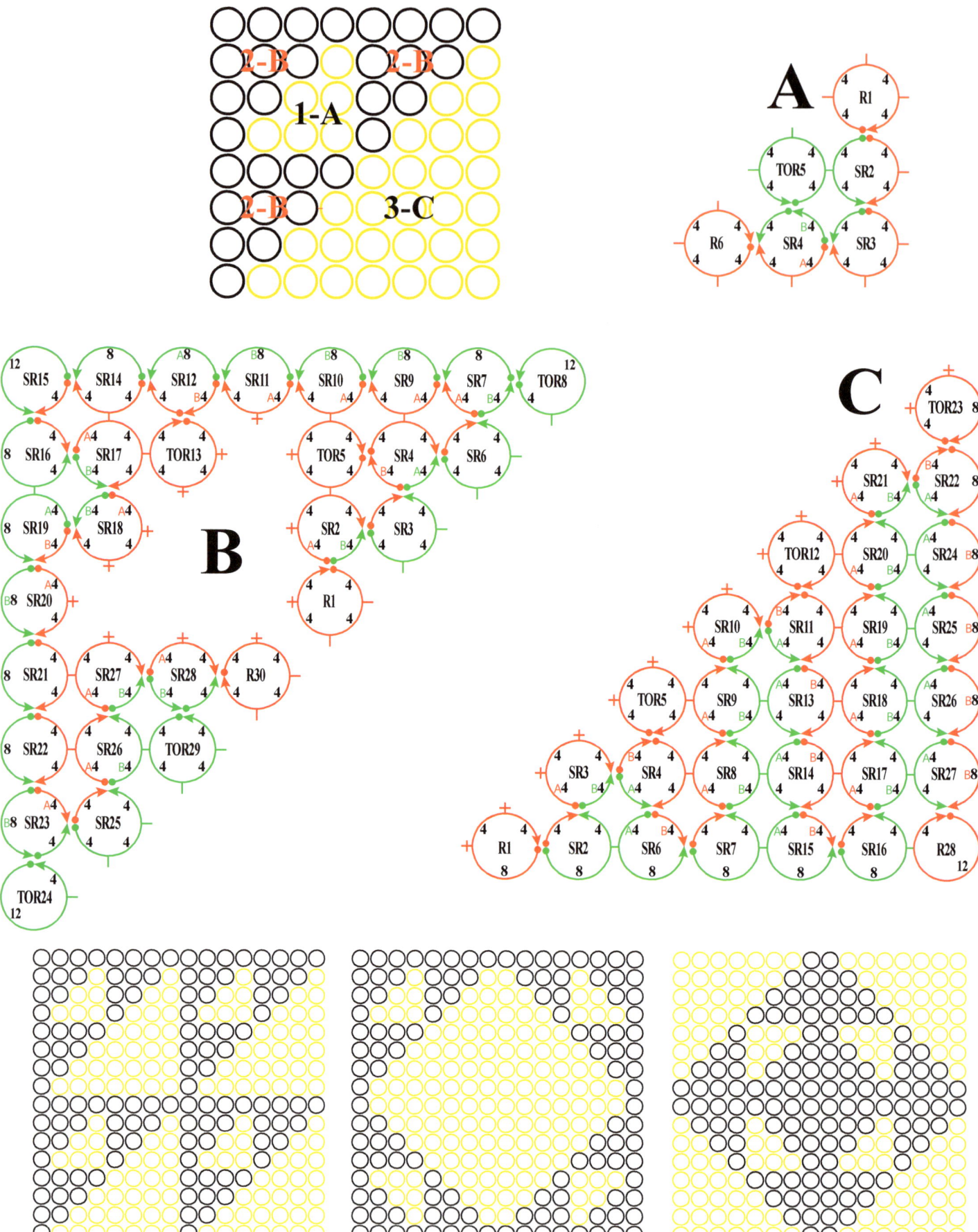

Whirling Geese

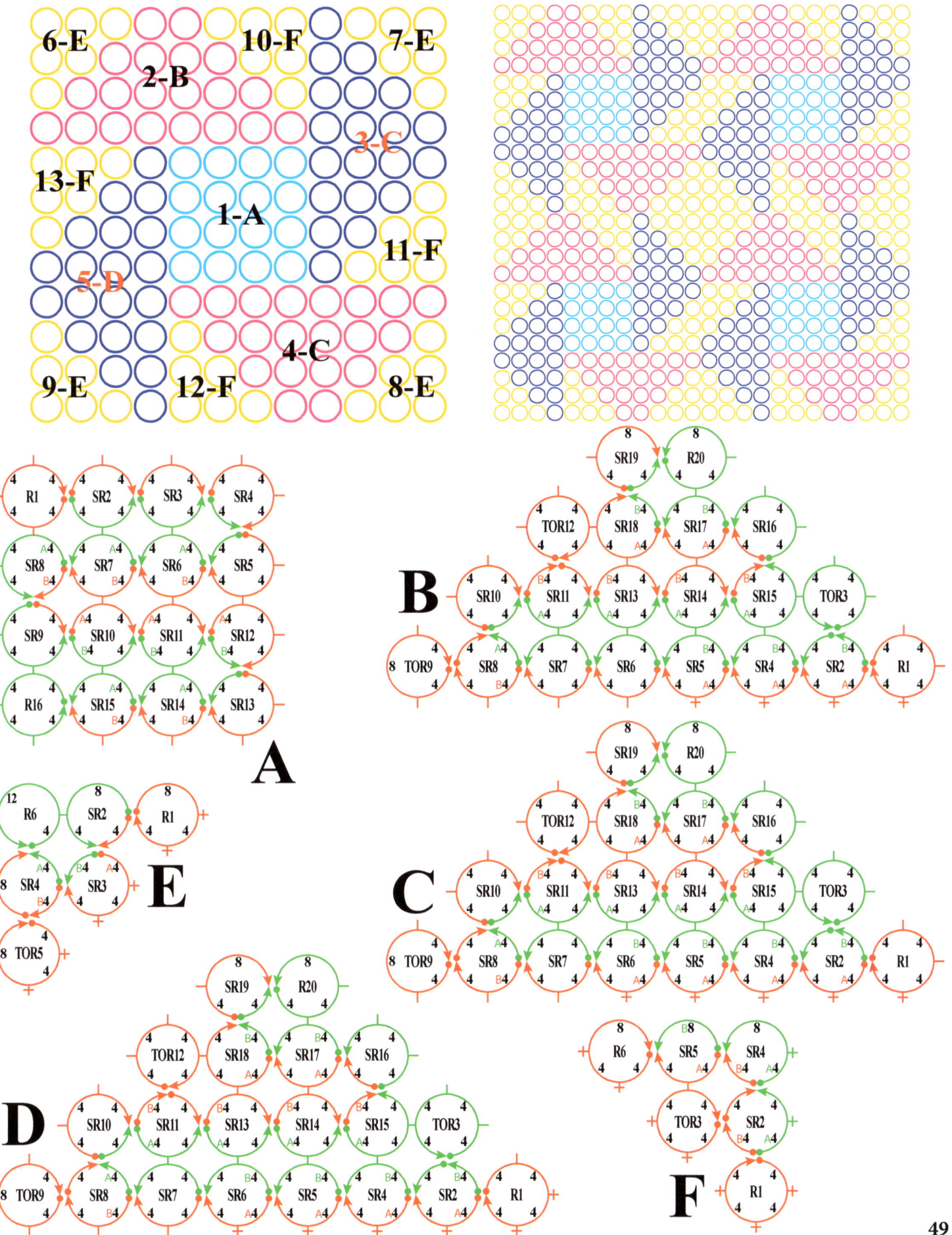

Maple Leaf

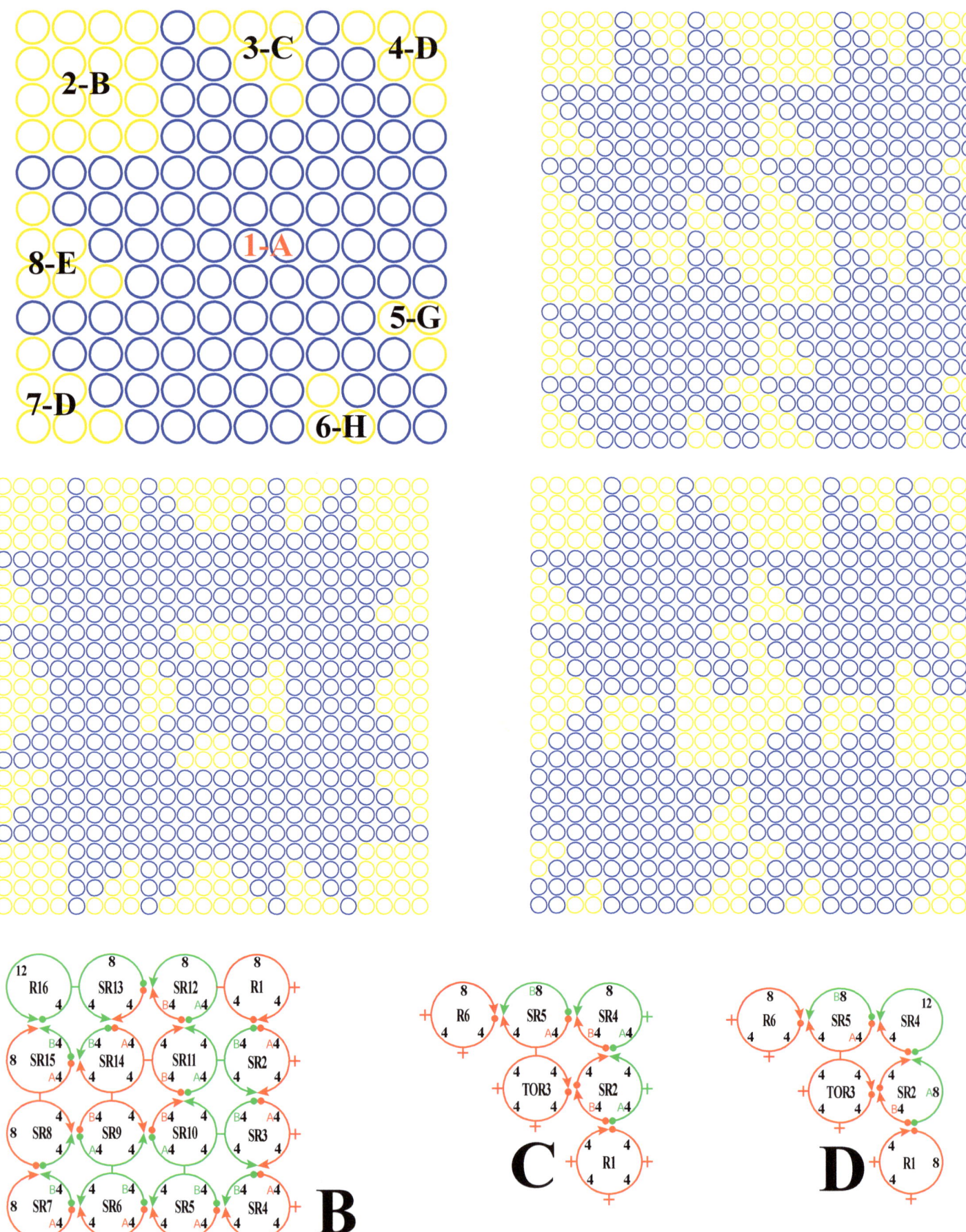

A

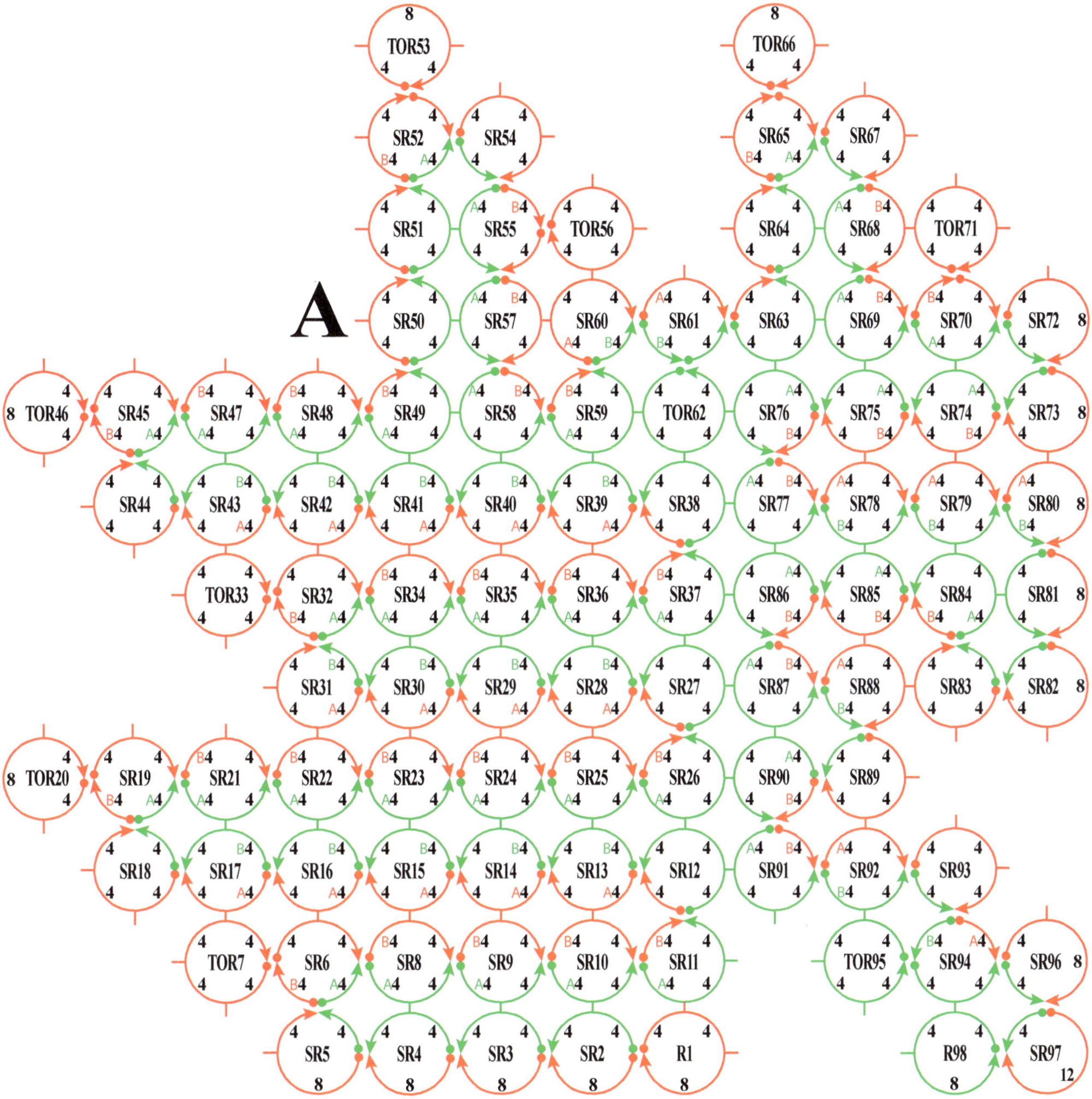
TOR53 TOR66
SR52 SR54 SR65 SR67
SR51 SR55 TOR56 SR64 SR68 TOR71
SR50 SR57 SR60 SR61 SR63 SR69 SR70 SR72
TOR46 SR45 SR47 SR48 SR49 SR58 SR59 TOR62 SR76 SR75 SR74 SR73
SR44 SR43 SR42 SR41 SR40 SR39 SR38 SR77 SR78 SR79 SR80
TOR33 SR32 SR34 SR35 SR36 SR37 SR86 SR85 SR84 SR81
SR31 SR30 SR29 SR28 SR27 SR87 SR88 SR83 SR82
TOR20 SR19 SR21 SR22 SR23 SR24 SR25 SR26 SR90 SR89
SR18 SR17 SR16 SR15 SR14 SR13 SR12 SR91 SR92 SR93
TOR7 SR6 SR8 SR9 SR10 SR11 TOR95 SR94 SR96
SR5 SR4 SR3 SR2 R1 R98 SR97

E

R6
SR4 TOR5
SR3 SR2 R1

G

R1 SR2
R3

H

R1
SR2 R3

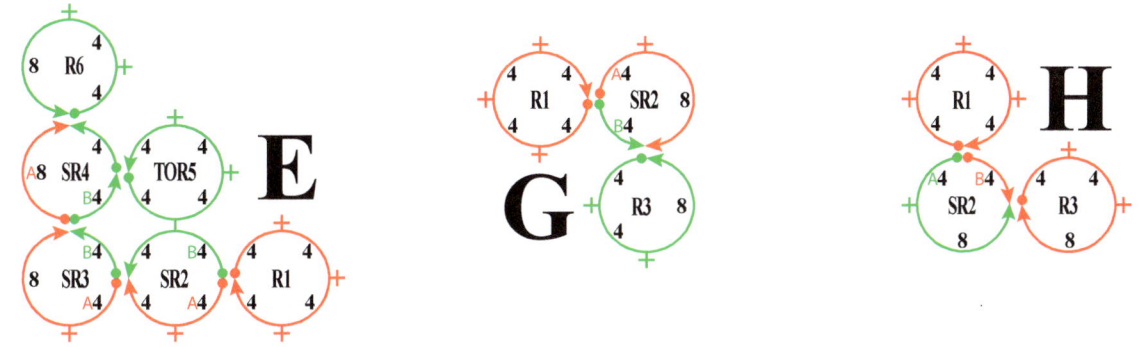

Album

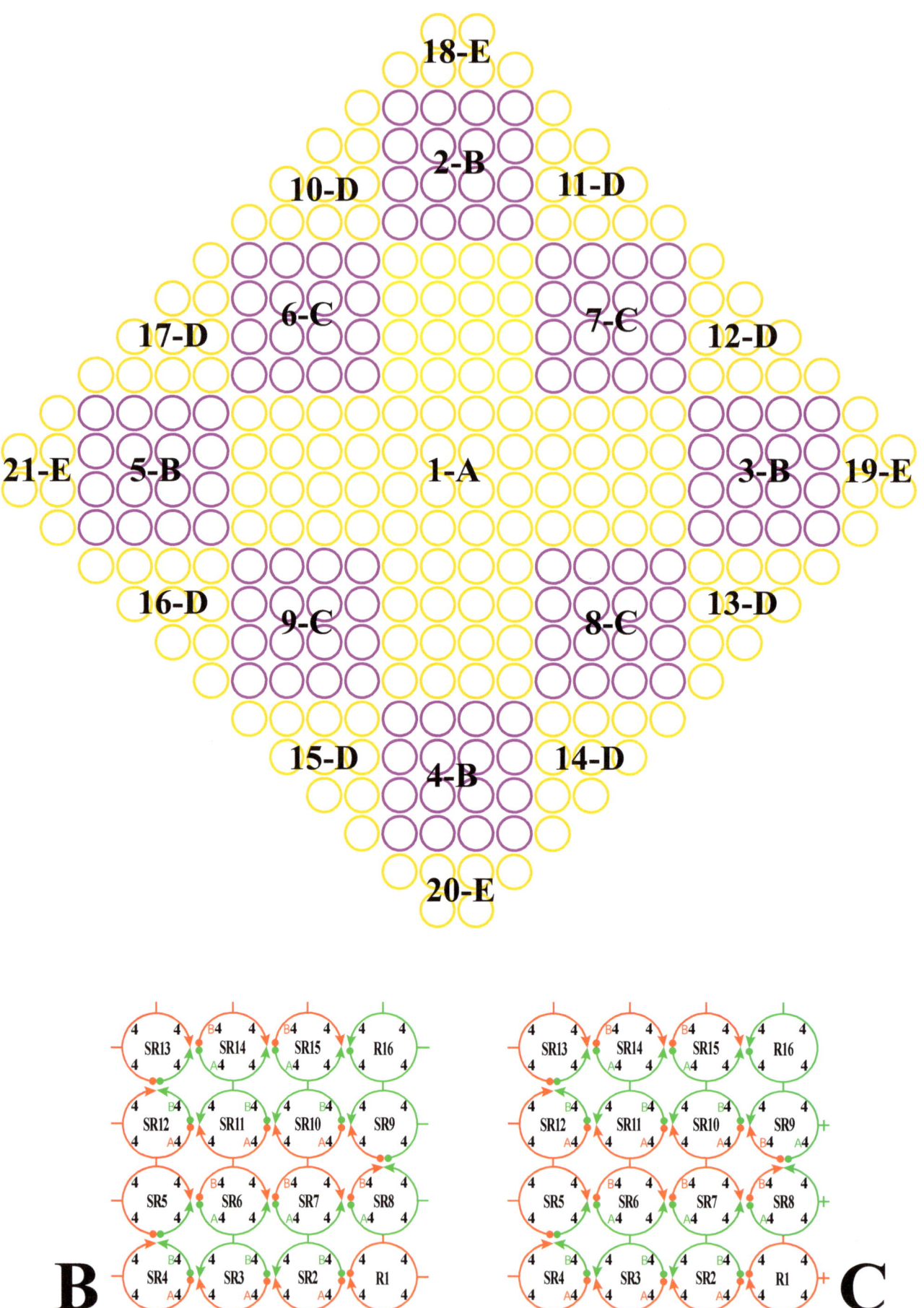

A

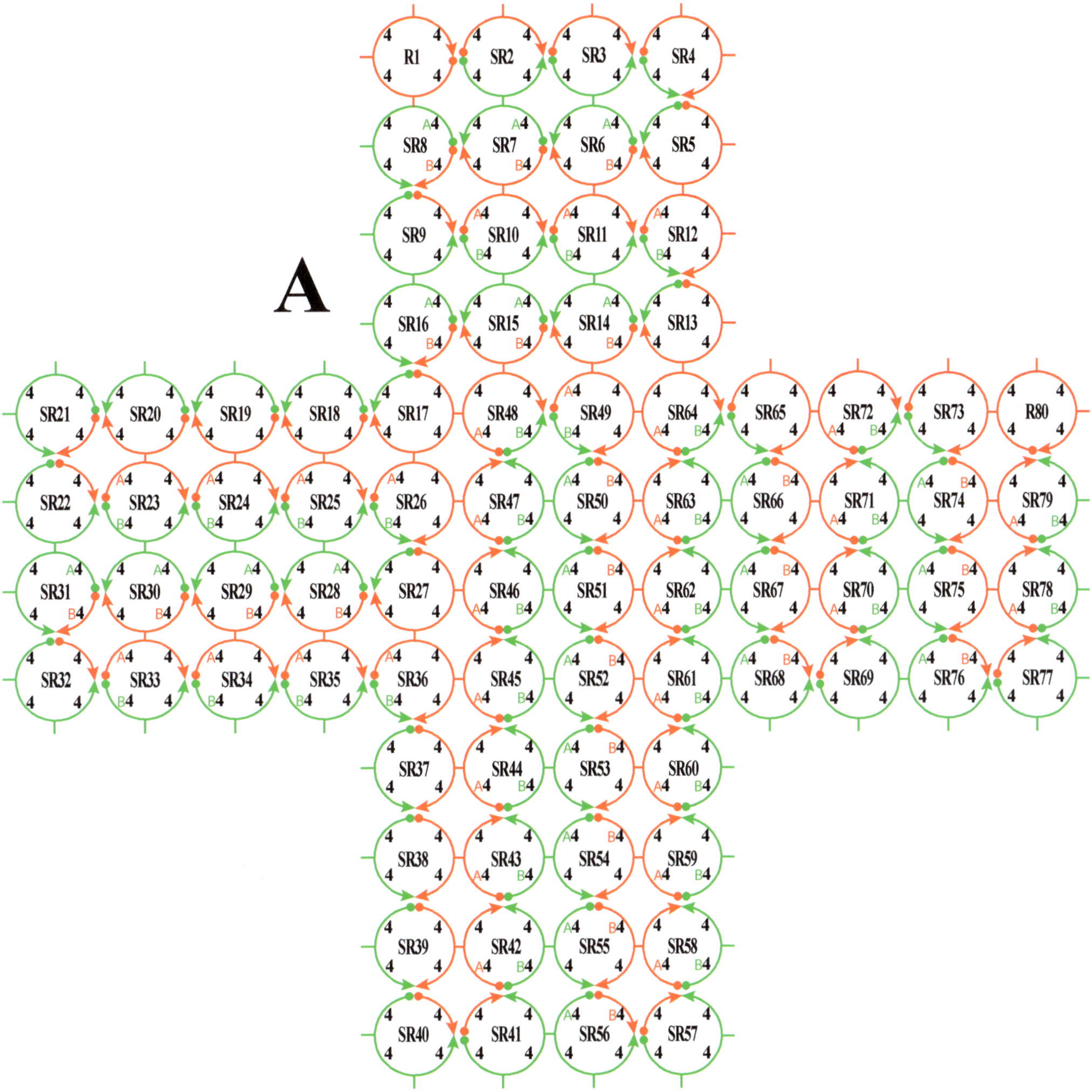
R1
SR2
SR3
SR4
SR8
SR7
SR6
SR5
SR9
SR10
SR11
SR12
SR16
SR15
SR14
SR13
SR21
SR20
SR19
SR18
SR17
SR48
SR49
SR64
SR65
SR72
SR73
R80
SR22
SR23
SR24
SR25
SR26
SR47
SR50
SR63
SR66
SR71
SR74
SR79
SR31
SR30
SR29
SR28
SR27
SR46
SR51
SR62
SR67
SR70
SR75
SR78
SR32
SR33
SR34
SR35
SR36
SR45
SR52
SR61
SR68
SR69
SR76
SR77
SR37
SR44
SR53
SR60
SR38
SR43
SR54
SR59
SR39
SR42
SR55
SR58
SR40
SR41
SR56
SR57

D

R10
SR8
SR9
TOR3
SR7
SR6
R1
SR2
SR4
SR5

E

TOR5
TOR3
R6
SR4
SR2
R1

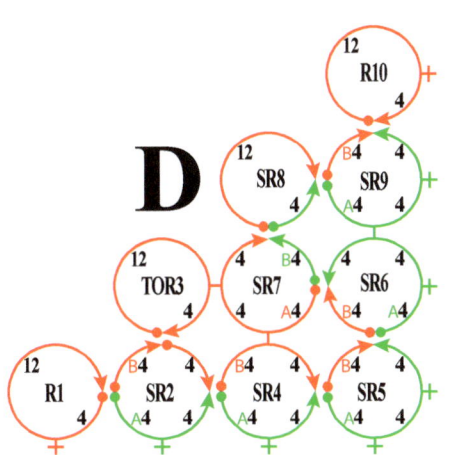

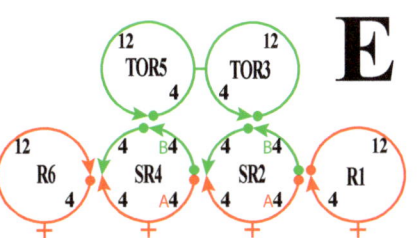

Double Star

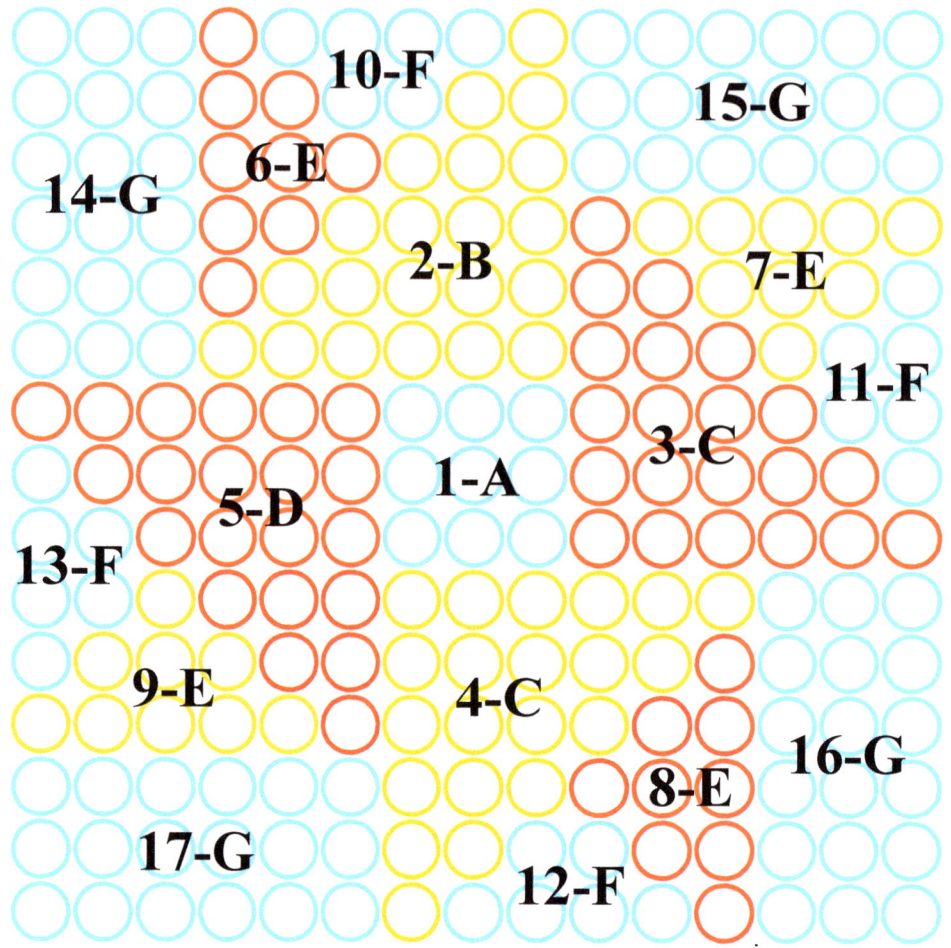

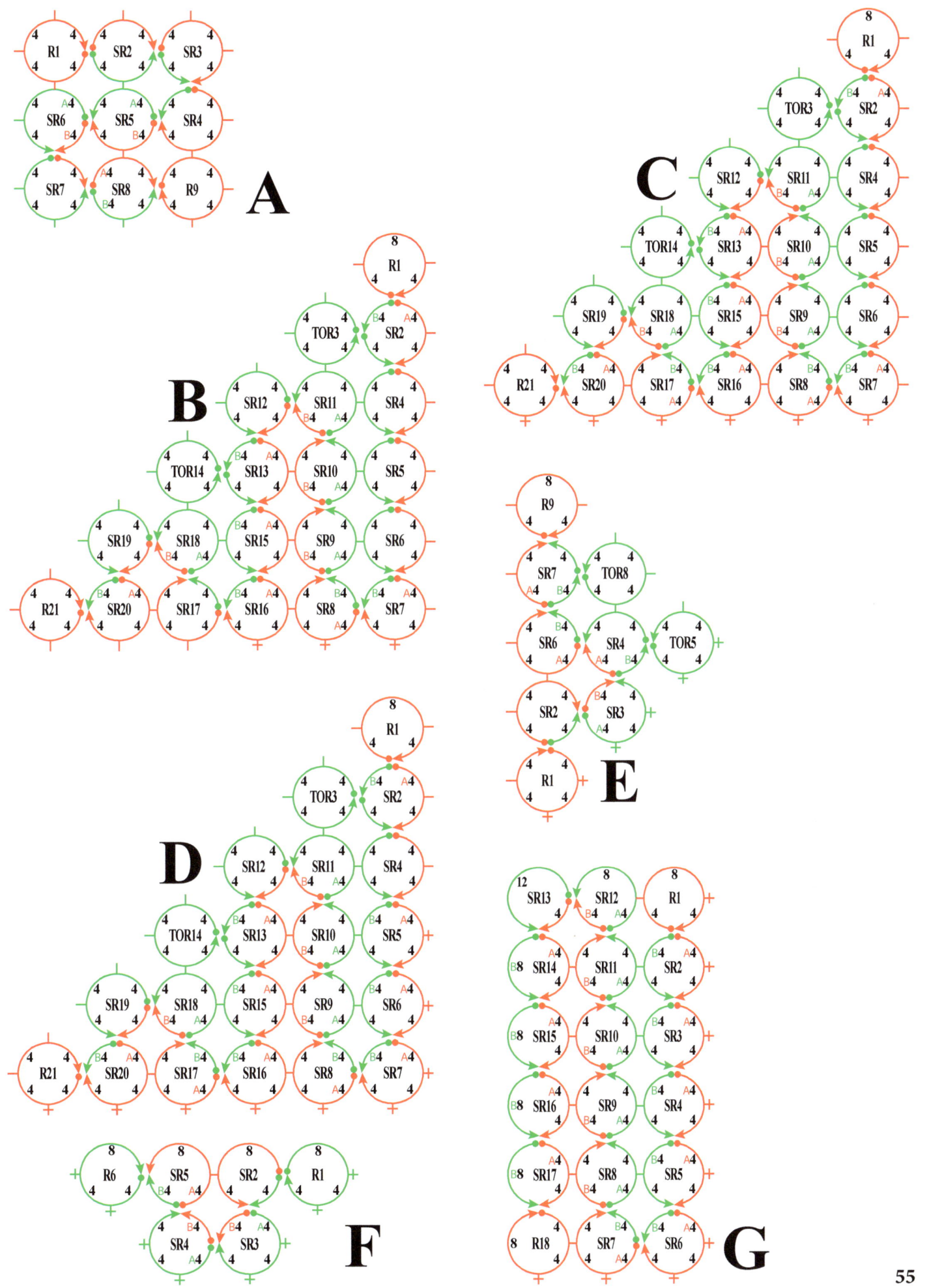

Tulips

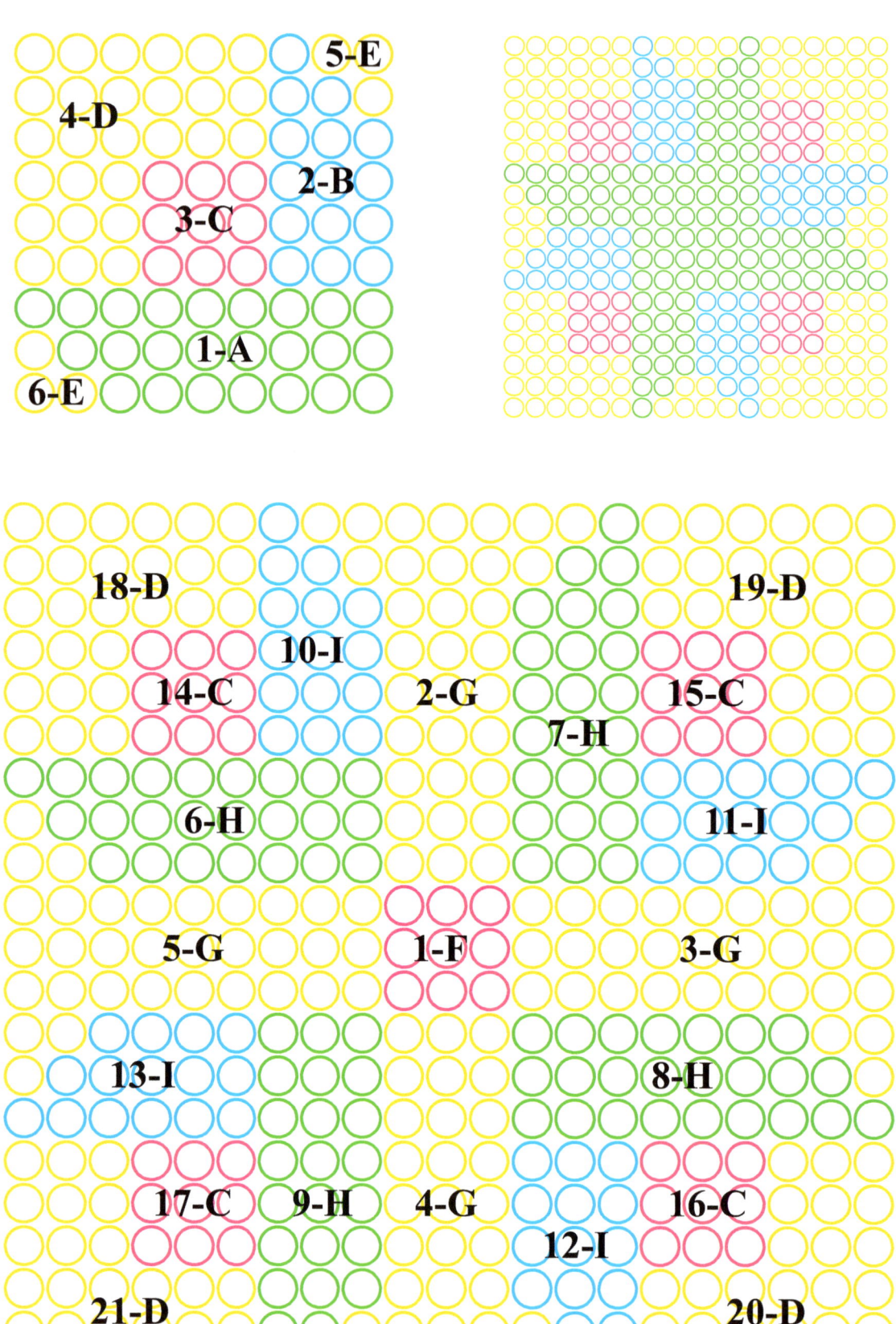

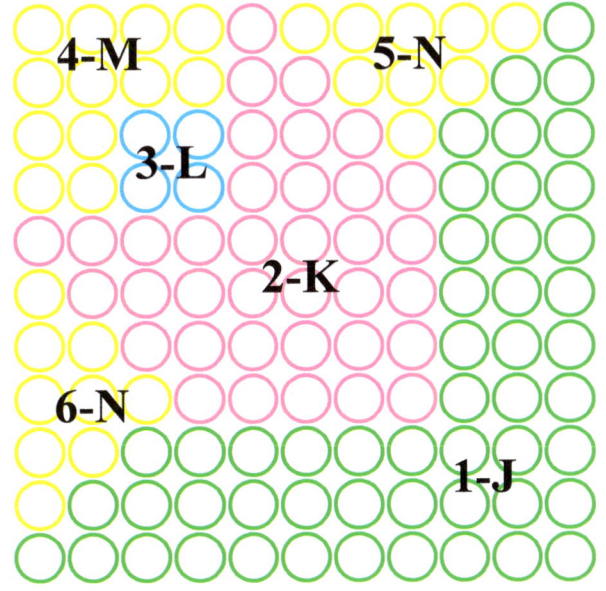
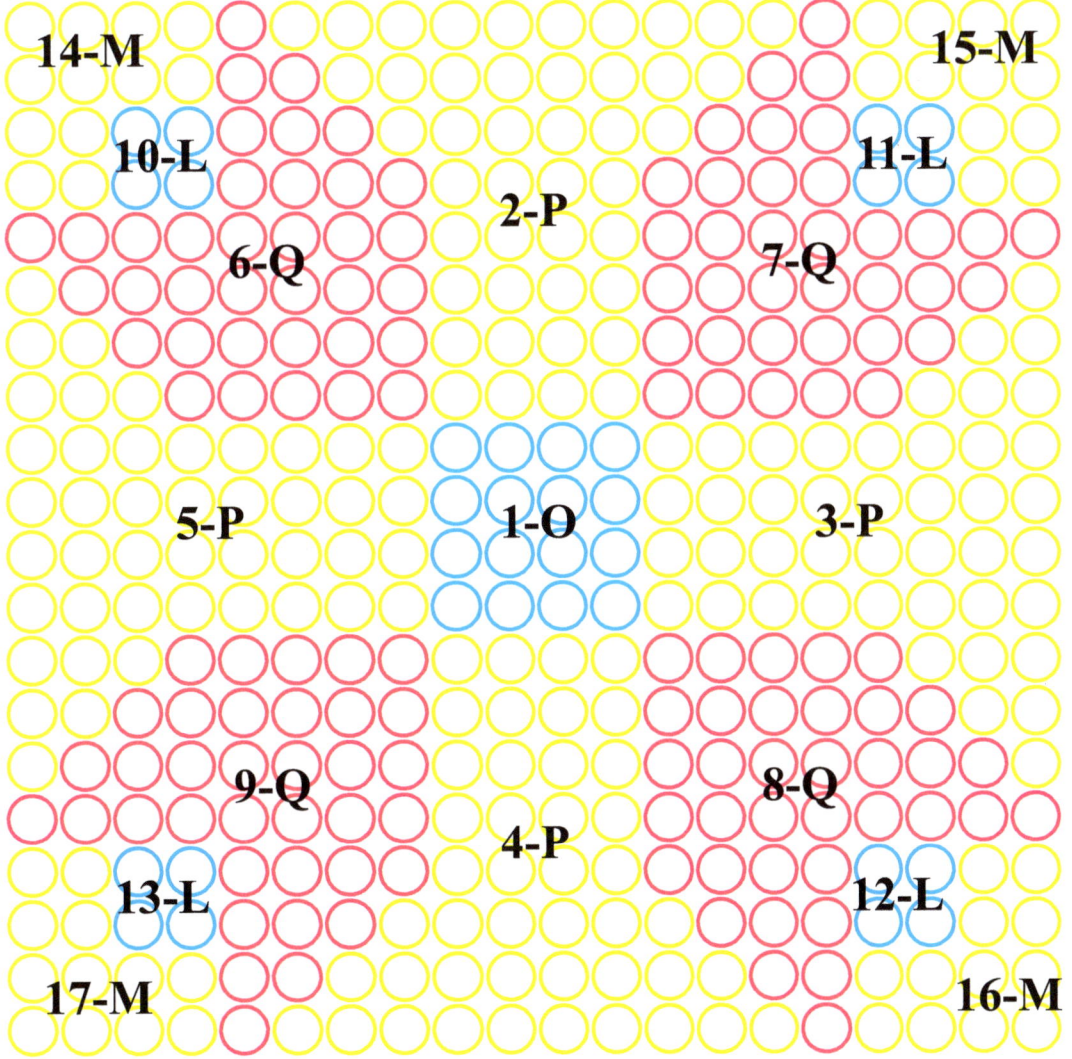

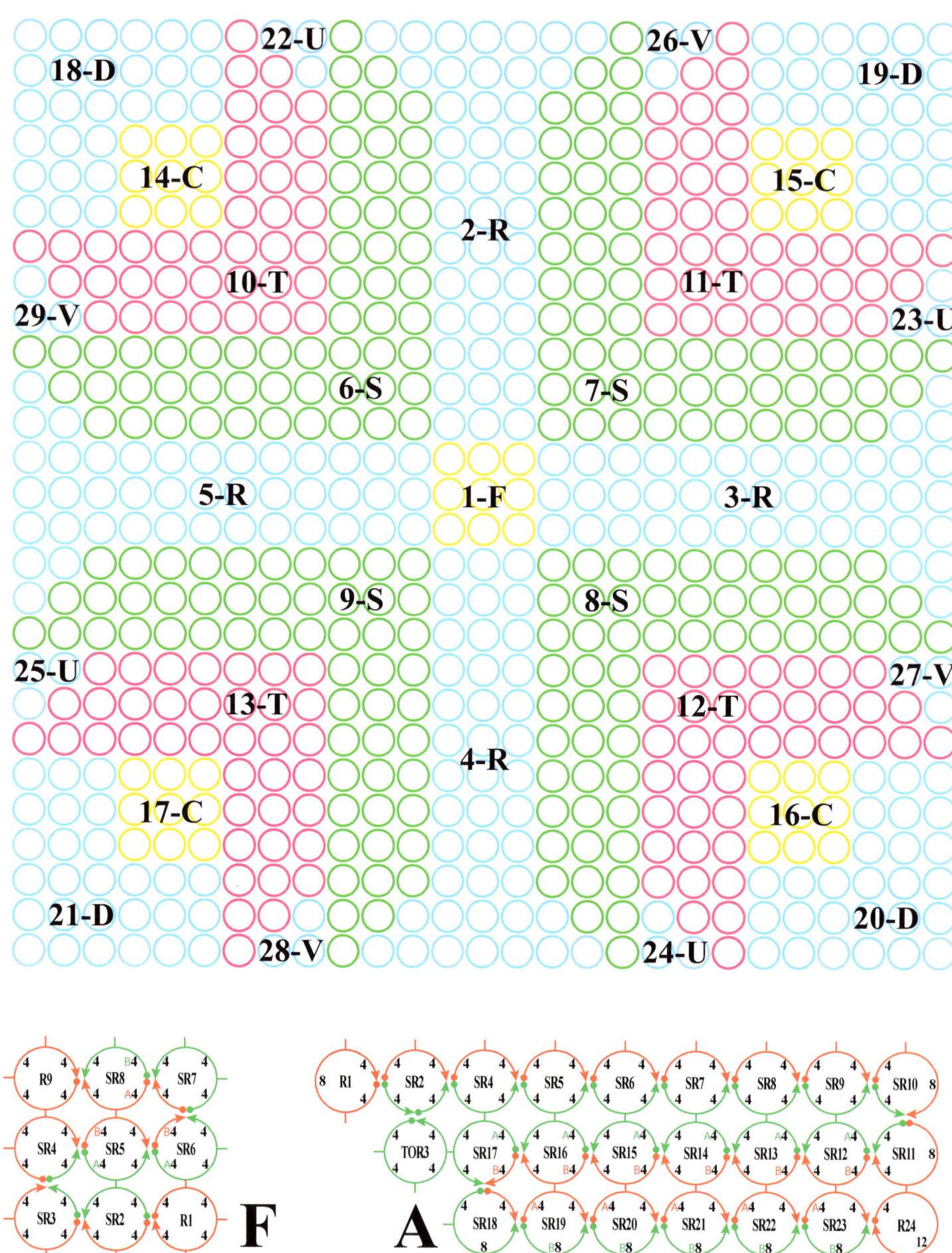

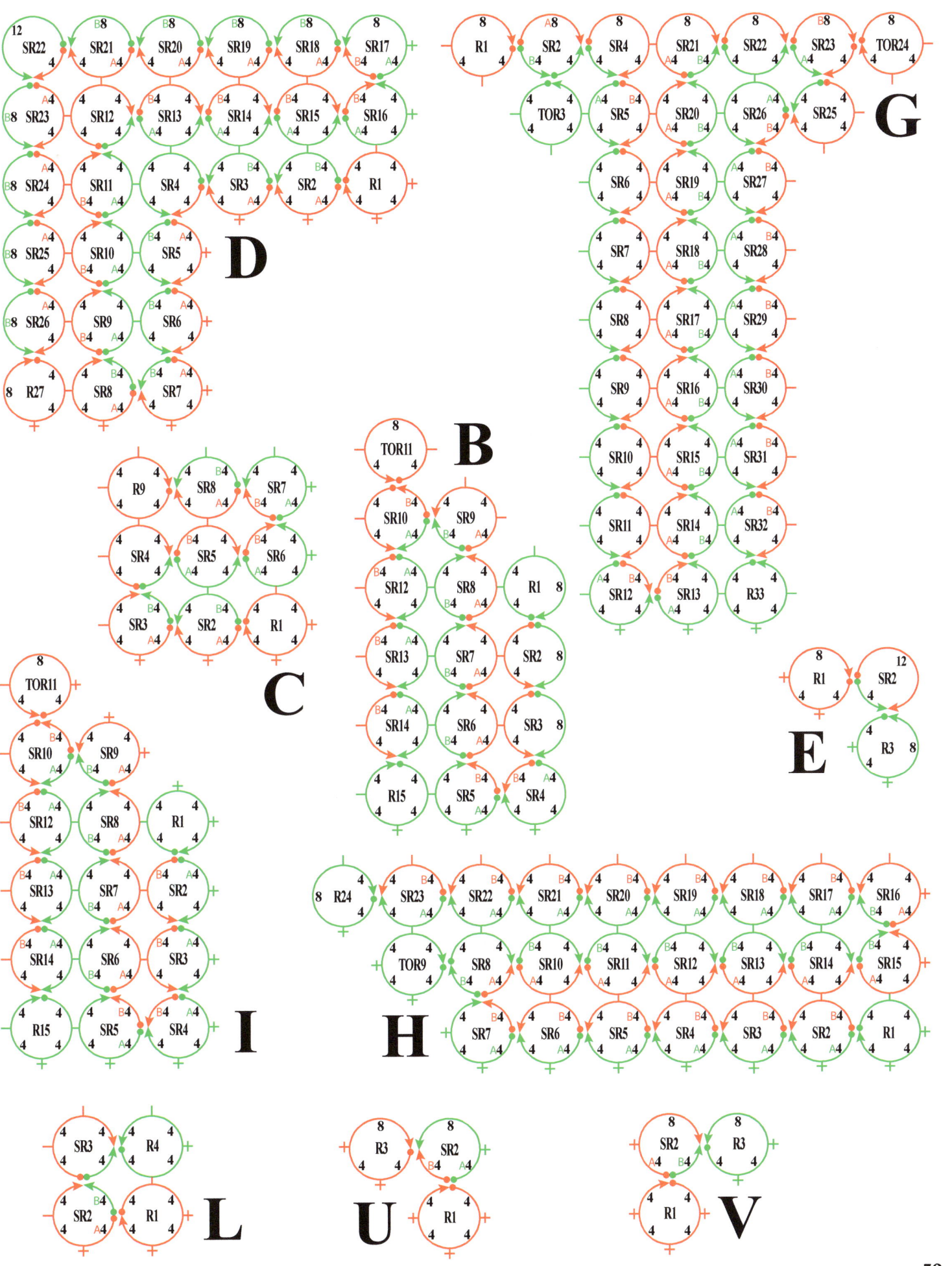

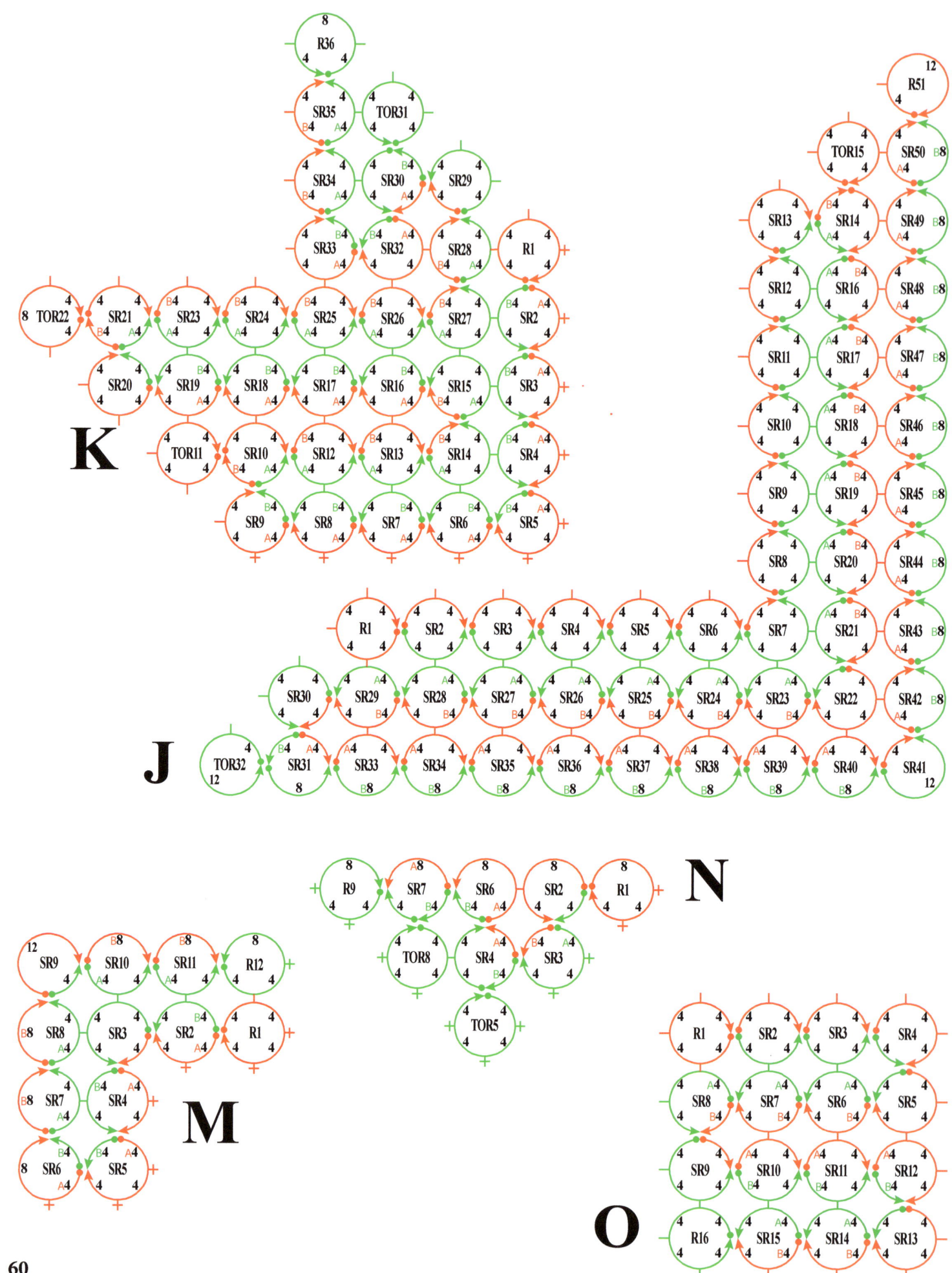

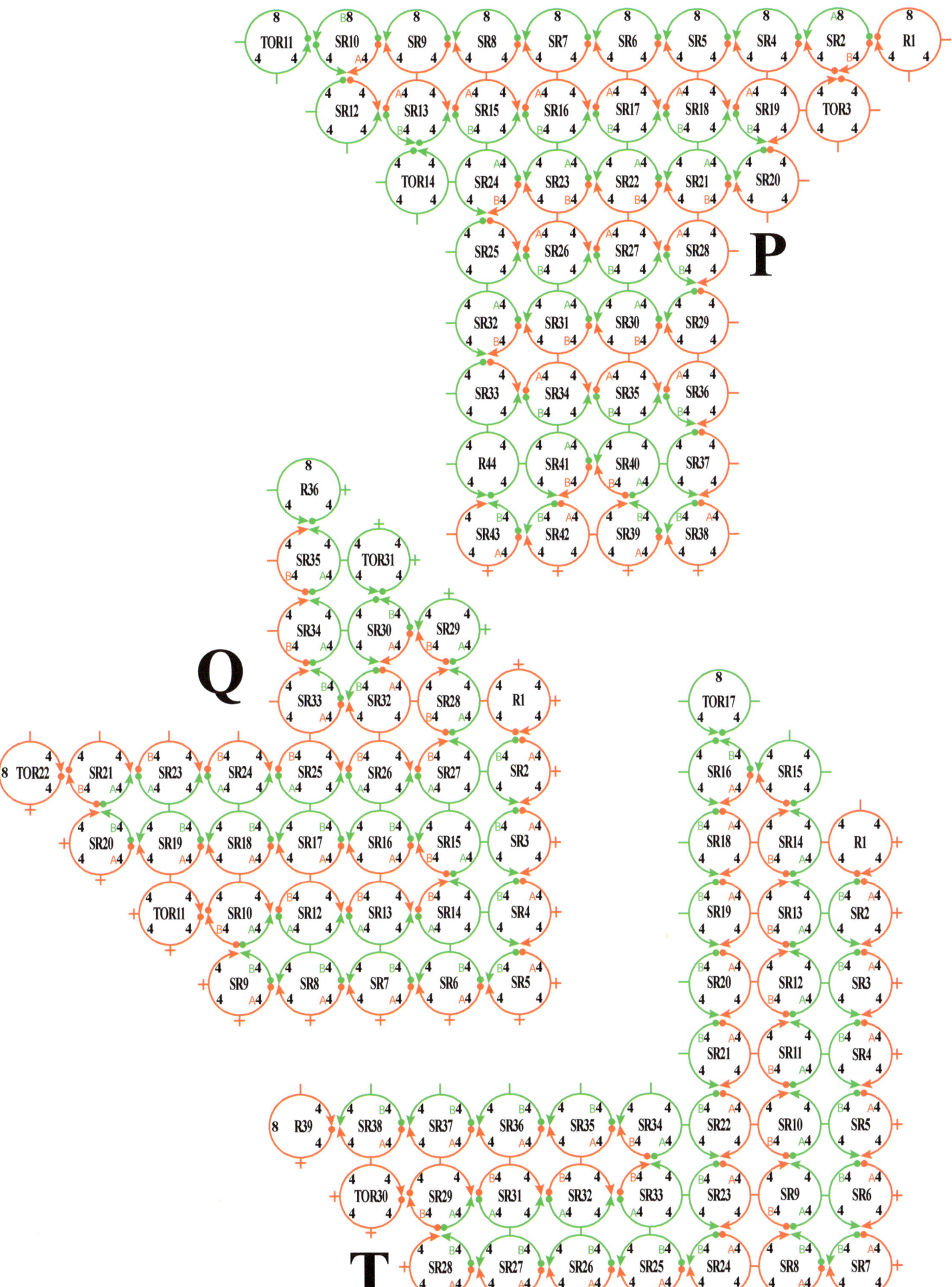

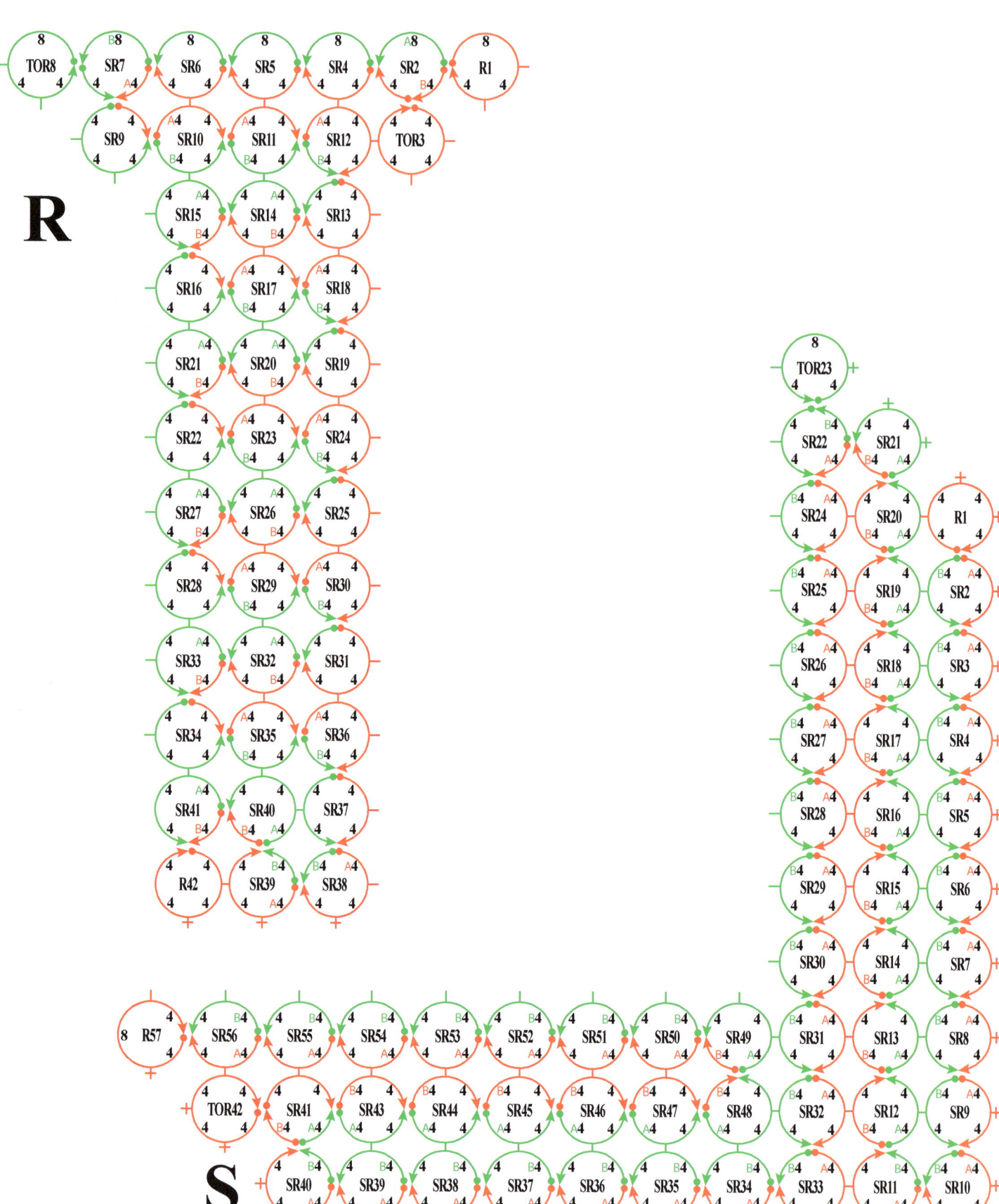

62

Walk in the Woods

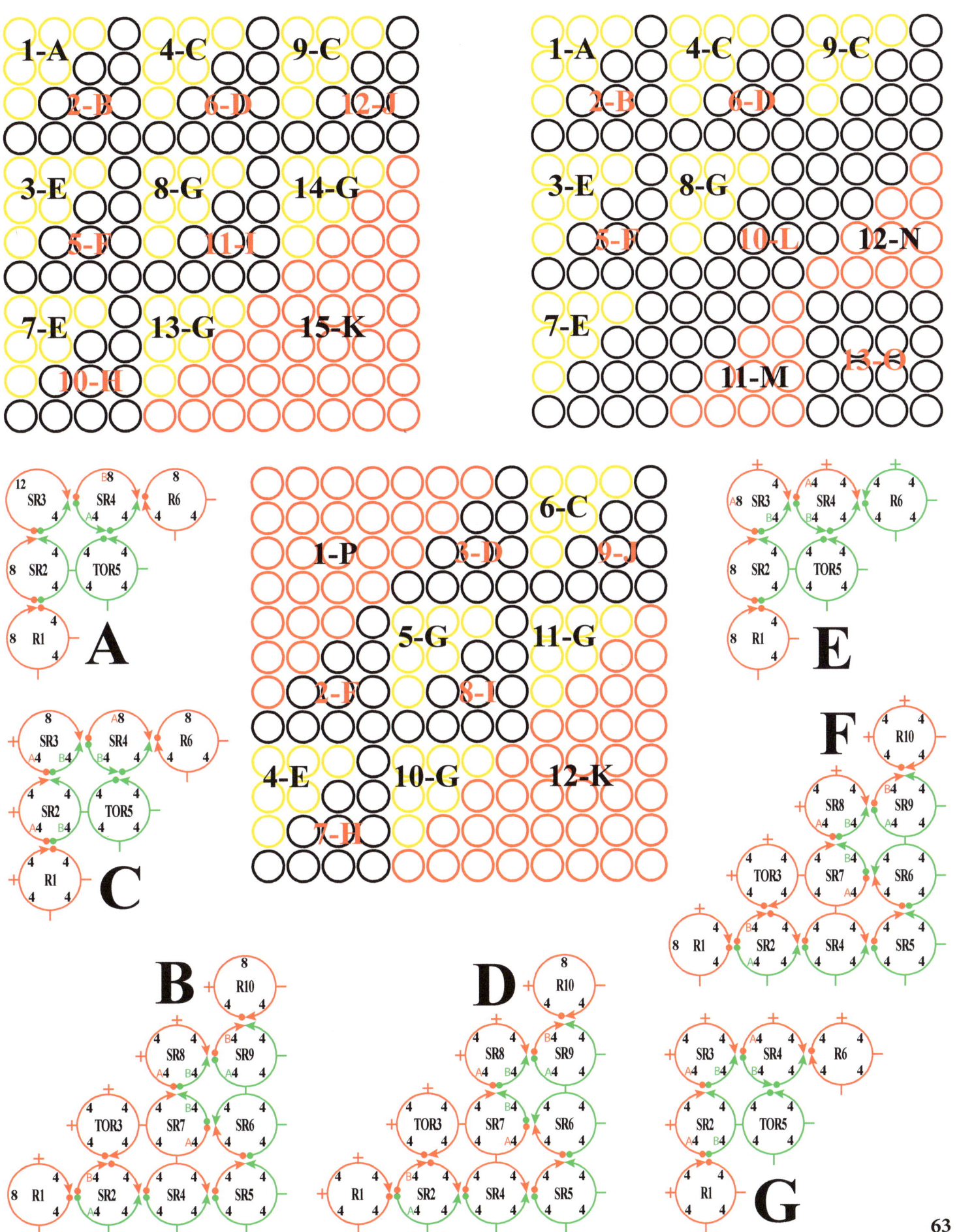

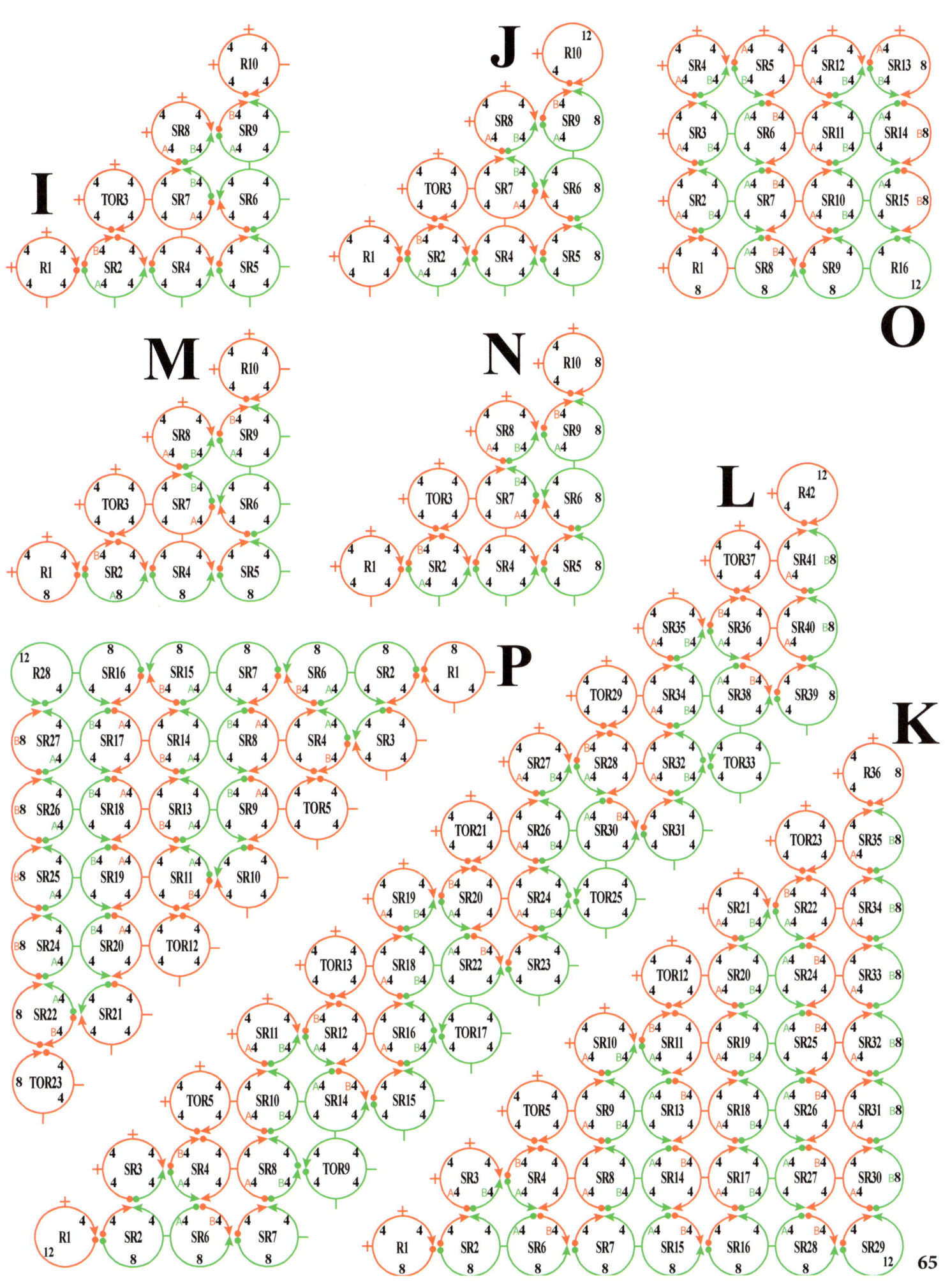

www.ingramcontent.com/pod-product-compliance
Lightning Source LLC
Chambersburg PA
CBHW042026150426
43198CB00002B/77